Political Leaders
of the
NSDAP

Edited by L. Milner

ALMARK PUBLISHING CO. LTD., LONDON

First published — August 1972

ISBN 0 85524 072 5 (hard cover edition)
ISBN 0 85524 073 3 (paper covered edition)

Printed in Great Britain by
Martins Press Ltd., London EC1R 0EN
for the publishers, Almark Publishing Co. Ltd.,
270 Burlington Road, New Malden,
Surrey KT3 4NL, England.

Introduction

ALTHOUGH much has been written about the National Socialist era, particularly in respect of military uniforms and decorations, little has so far been published dealing in detail with the so-called Political Leaders of the Nazi Party. The intention of this book is to provide the serious uniform enthusiast—as well as students of the history of the Third Reich—with an illustrated record of the various orders of dress, badges, insignia, and decorations of all the grades of Political Leader. In order to make the complexities of the ranks and grades intelligible it is also necessary to give some account of the organization, functions, selection, qualifications, and indoctrination of Political Leaders.

The subject of the National Socialist Party is still politically sensitive in most areas and rather than offer personal comment or trying to unravel the immense subject of Nazi organization here, we have instead presented the entire book in the Nazi Party's own words. The text which follows is an exact translation of the section dealing with Political Leaders and the Dress of Political Leaders from the Nazi Party's own rule book, the *Organisationsbuch der NSDAP* (Organization Book of the National Socialist Party), 1943 edition. Some other items dealing with the organization side are also reproduced from this book. Though a facsimile edition of the complete *Organisationsbuch der NSDAP* is available from an American publisher, this is in the original German Gothic text, difficult to read even for the modern non-German who knows the language. Much of the original book is taken up with highly detailed administrative information of only limited interest to the uniform enthusiast; this present volume reproduces the uniform section in English at a more modest price. It must be pointed out, however, that the actual translated text has not been altered in any way from its original style or wordage, as the editor and publishers feel that the National Socialist platitudes contained herein give some indication of the social climate of the period in Nazi Germany; in the case of the stated qualities expected of a Political Leader the text gives an interesting (and sinister) insight into the type of person that the Führer, Adolf Hitler, fondly imagined he had at his disposal.

The *Organisationsbuch*, being in effect the handbook for Political Leaders at all levels, dealt fully with all aspects of their work, and the 1943 edition was chosen in this instance because it was felt that the uniform plates here

CONTENTS

Organisationsbuch der NSDAP.

1943

Herausgeber:

Der Reichsorganisationsleiter der NSDAP.

Zentralverlag der NSDAP., Franz Eher Nachf., München

illustrated would reproduce better than the poorer quality plates of earlier editions. Also, the 1943 edition was the most 'complete' in terms of text and coverage.

Organization

In most cases when writing about military or para-military organizations of the Third Reich, one can draw parallels with British or American military formations to clarify points of organization, details, and ranks and specializations. Not so with the Political Leadership of the NSDAP, however, as this was, in effect, a uniformed local government at its lowest level, and a uniformed ministerial cabinet (without any opposition party) at its highest level.

The Politische Leitung (Political Leadership) of the NSDAP was comprised of four main levels, which are briefly explained here:

Reichpleitung: Subordinate directly to the Führer, the highest level of leadership included departments concerned with Organization, Education, Personnel, Finance, Propaganda, and Jurisdiction (all of which also existed at other levels) and in addition there were departments dealing with Foreign Policy, Foreign Press Party Censorship, Party Archives, Colonial Policy, the Reichstag Nazi Faction, and the department of the Führer's Representatives (Beautrager des Führers) for the control of Political and Ideological education of the Party.

Gauleitung: A Gau was an administrative district led by a Gauleiter and his staff. By 1943 there were 43 Gaue in Germany including the Auslands-organisation (AO) which was comprised of Party members living outside the frontiers of 'Greater Germany' and which had the status of a Gau.

Kreisleitung: Each Gau was sub-divided into several Kreise (Sub-Administrative District) of which there were 920 each led by a Kreisleiter and his staff. The Political Leaders at Kreis level were the lowest ranking paid officials in the Party, those at the lower levels being part-time and not, in fact, paid for their services.

Ortsgruppenleitung: Each Kreis was again sub-divided into several Ortsgruppen (local groups) each led by an Ortsgruppenleiter and his staff, each controlling several Zellen (cells), each of which in turn controlled several Blocks. The Blockleiter was thus responsible for 40 to 60 households, and kept an index (Haushaltskarten) about them all, assessing their attitudes to the Party and the state. Regular reports were sent to the Block and so on through the structure. Thus any unrest was dealt with at source and the NSDAP wielded absolute control throughout the state.

Each Gau and Kreis had a Schulungsamt (Department of Education) which was responsible for the ideological training of Political Leaders and the most promising students from these schools were sent to one of the three Ordens-burgen situated at Krossinsee in Pomerania, Southhofein in the Bavarian Alps, and Vogelsang in the Eifel. The name Ordensburg was taken from the castles of the Teutonic knights and the students were known as Junkers. Early in 1943 the first course of instruction was opened at Krossinsee for selected disabled soldiers who were to be given Party appointments to replace other Party officials serving with the armed forces.

Comparative Ranks

Although it is impossible to translate the purely political ranks of the Politische Leitung into English, one can compare them in some ways to military rank and the following table gives a rough approximation of equivalents:

Army Rank (*British given*)	Politische Leitung Rank
Private	{ Anwärter
	{ Helfer
Lance-Corporal	{ Oberhelfer
	{ Arbeitsleiter
Corporal	Oberarbeitsleiter
Sergeant	Hauptarbeitsleiter
Staff-Sergeant	Bereitschaftsleiter
Sergeant-Major	Oberbereitschaftsleiter
Regimental Sergeant-Major	Hauptbereitschaftsleiter
Second Lieutenant	{ Einsatzleiter
	{ Obereinsatzleiter
Lieutenant	{ Haupteinsatzleiter
	{ Gemeinschaftsleiter
Captain	{ Obergemeinschaftsleiter
	{ Hauptgemeinschaftsleiter
Major	{ Abschnittsleiter
	{ Oberabschnittsleiter
Lieutenant-Colonel	{ Hauptabschnittsleiter
	{ Bereichsleiter
Colonel	{ Oberbereichsleiter
	{ Hauptbereichsleiter
Brigadier	{ Dienstleiter
	{ Oberdienstleiter
Major-General	Hauptdienstleiter
Lieutenant-General	Befehlshaber
General	{ Oberbefehlshaber
	{ Gauleiter
Field-Marshal	{ Hauptbefehlsleiter
	{ Reichsleiter

We would like to thank Mr. P. J. Simkins of the Department of Exhibits, Imperial War Museum, London, for permission to photograph the Political Leader's cap from the Museum's collection. Mr. J. S. Lucas of the Imperial War Museum Library helped with many of the technical and political terms in the translation and thanks are due to him and to Mr. Matthew Cooper, who helped in selecting photographs and providing additional background material for this present volume.

All relevant illustrations from the *Organisationsbuch* are included, all the most important ones in colour. Most are reproduced smaller than the original for reasons of space. A few original colour plates are shown in half-tone only, again for space reasons. Additional pictures are chosen to show examples of dress in everyday use. These are provided specially for this volume and were not in the original *Organisationsbuch*.

The layout and style of the text follows as closely as possible the style of the original German text, headings and sub-headings included.

Dr Josef Goebbels in Linz, wearing the service dress uniform of a Gauleiter. He was Gauleiter of Berlin as well as Reichsminister for Propaganda. Note the leather military-style overcoat which is not covered in the official regulations.

LEFT: Reichsleiter Walter Funk in the regulation walking out dress (Uniform 4c) with light brown jacket. He wears the Golden Badge of Honour among his decorations. ABOVE: Dr Hugo Jury, Gauleiter of Niederdonau, presenting War Service Crosses to factory workers. Note the armband and collar patch of the Gauleiter rank.

Der Politische Leiter

Grundlage der Organisation der Partei ist der Führergedanke. Die Allgemeinheit kann sich nicht selbst regieren, weder mittel- noch unmittelbar. Führer soll sein, wer am besten dazu geeignet ist. Der wird auch vom Vertrauen des Volkes getragen. Alle Politischen Leiter gelten als vom Führer ernannt und sind ihm verantwortlich, sie genießen nach unten **volle Autorität**. Bei der Auswahl der Politischen Leiter kommt es darauf an, den richtigen Mann an die richtige Stelle zu setzen. Die Ämter der Partei sind derartig verschieden, daß es großer Menschenkenntnis und langjähriger Erfahrung bedarf, um die Führerauslese richtig zu treffen. Alter, gesellschaftliche Stellung sind nebensächlich, **Charakter und Eignung entscheiden allein**. Grundsätzlich ist dabei zu beachten: **Nur wer durch die Schule der Kleinarbeit in unserer Partei gegangen ist, darf bei entsprechender Eignung Anspruch auf höhere Führerämter erheben.** Wir können nur Führer brauchen, die von der Pike auf gedient haben. **Jeder Politische Leiter, der von diesem Grundsatz abweicht, soll entfernt werden** oder zur Ausbildung an die unteren Arbeitsgebiete (als Blockleiter, Zellenleiter) zurückverwiesen werden.

Jeder Politische Leiter sei sich als politischer F ü h r e r vom ersten bis zum letzten bewußt, daß Führertum nicht nur mehr Rechte gibt, sondern in erster Linie höhere Pflichten auferlegt.

Die erste Pflicht des Politischen Leiters ist, ein Vorbild im persönlichen Auftreten, in der Dienstauffassung und im außerdienstlichen Leben zu sein. Er ist sich dessen bewußt, daß ein schlechtes Beispiel des Politischen Leiters mehr schadet, als hundert Ermahnungen gutmachen können. Der Block, die Zelle, die Ortsgruppe, der Kreis und der Gau sind immer das Spiegelbild ihres Hoheitsträgers. Wer in seinem Heimatort oder Wohnbereich nichts leistet, wird auch anderswo versagen.

Die zweite Pflicht ist **unbedingte Gerechtigkeit**. Jede Vetternwirtschaft hat zu unterbleiben. Wer tüchtige Parteigenossen nicht aufkommen läßt, weil er Angst hat, sie könnten ihn ausstechen, ist ein erbärmlicher Wicht und ein Schädling der Partei. Der Hoheitsträger muß nicht alles allein machen wollen. Er muß der Richtunggebende, der Überwachende, der Schlichtende, mit einem Wort: die Seele des Ganzen sein. Aus Sorgen um seine Gruppe, in vielen Fällen sein Werk, muß der Politische Leiter jeden Funken Zündstoff, der sich zeigt, augenblicklich auslöschen. Er muß vorausschauen und nicht nachhinken. Aus all diesen Gründen darf er sich nicht mit Kleinarbeit überlasten.

Jede Führerstellung erfordert ein erhebliches Maß an Wissen und Können. Deshalb muß sich jeder Politische Leiter dauernd weiterbilden, und die Partei sieht es als ihre vornehmste Aufgabe an, eine dau-

The Political Leader

THE basis of Party organization is the Leadership principle. The mass of the people cannot rule themselves either directly or indirectly. Only those who are suitable should lead and such persons enjoy the trust of the people. All Political Leaders must feel that they have been selected by the Führer and that they are responsible to him. They have complete authority over their subordinates. When selecting Political Leaders it is important to have the right man in the right job. The Departments of the Party are of such a diverse nature that it requires a great knowledge of human nature and many years of experience to be able to select the correct person. Social considerations are unimportant. Character and suitability are the only deciding factors. It should be a general rule that only he who has passed through the school of experience can, if otherwise suitable, lay claim to senior positions of leadership in our Party. We can use as leaders only those who have risen from the ranks. Any Political Leader who departs from this principle must be removed or returned for training to a junior area of authority (eg, as a Block Leader, or a Cell Leader.)

Every Political Leader must be aware, from first to last, that a position of authority does not only bestow privileges, but, more important, carries with it high responsibilities.

The first duty of a Political Leader is to be an example in his personal appearance, in the execution of his duty and in his personal life. He must be aware that one bad example as a Political Leader does more harm than a hundred exhortations can make good. From the lowest area of authority to the regional leadership, all offices are the mirror of thier incumbent. The man who fails to do his duty in his own home town or locality is the man who will fail everywhere else.

The second duty is absolute justice and impartiality. Every sort of nepotism is to be avoided. The man who refuses to promote an able Party member because he fears that such a promotion might threaten his own position, is a miserable wretch and damages the Party. The man in authority must not try to do everything himself. He it is who must give the necessary direction, he must be the supervisor, the arbitrator—in one word the soul, the motivating force of of the whole. Because he cares so much for his Group, which is in many cases his Work, the Political Leader must extinguish, immediately, anything inflammatory. He must look ahead and not look back. For all these reasons he must allow himself to be overloaded with petty details.

Every position of authority demands an inordinate amount of knowledge and ability. Therefore each Political Leader must continue his education and the Party must see it as one of its most satisfactory duties to make possible the continuing education of its Political Leaders. It is not the commission which makes the leader, but the fact that his subordinates are able to look up to him under every circumstance. Not every Political Leader is a gifted speaker, but each must be a preacher, a propagandist of the idea.

Each Political Leader must have strength of character. Do your duty wherever you are called upon to serve. If you are in the ranks of the infantry you cannot serve on the General Staff and vice-versa.

Concern yourself with your duties, but do not accept more offices than you can manage; but manage those you have, completely. If a Political Leader wishes to carry out his appointed tasks correctly and thoroughly then he must not allow his strength to be dissipated. He should not become a member of private societies and, more important still, he should take no part in their administration.

Each public appearance as a representative of the Party, or indeed, any intra-mural function, eg, instructional classes, lectures in oratory, meetings of members, etc, must be most carefully planned. If you have instructions to give then give them briefly and exactly. Never say: 'I think, one should, or it would be better if.' Your opinion is superfluous. On the contrary, those present want to know your mind and your intention. By this way they become part of the collective responsibility and there is no more room for doubt.

Always remember: The man who is unable to obey will never be able to give an order. Never put forward your own personal point of view. There is only one point of view; that of the Movement. Take care to maintain liaison with all other branches of the Party.

The Type of Political Leaders

FROM all of this there arises the ideal Political Leader type. A Political Leader is not an official but the political representative of the Leader. He has to think and to see clearly. He has to be the people's anchor in times of crisis and give absolute obedience. It is upon the Political Leader that we can build political leadership within the state.

The Political Leader must be both Preacher and Soldier at one and the same time.

He must never become a Bureaucrat but must always be active among and for the people. He must be an example.

Common sense is the product of instinct and understanding. It is not important that a Political Leader has every fact at his finger-tips (he has aides for this purpose), but his decision must be the decisive one. The Political Leader type is not characterized by the office he holds. There are, for example, no Political Leaders within the NSBO—there are only

Political Leaders of the NSDAP

Political Leader Candidates

In the local and district administration of the NSDAP, Party members and, where necessary, even non-Party members, who are suited to become Political Leaders and who fulfil the Party membership conditions, can be selected as a Political Leader candidate.

For details of those authorized to wear Political Leader candidate uniform and the appropriate badges of office, see the details on page 26H of the Organizations book,* under the chapter entitled 'Uniform for Political Leader Candidates'.

---

* See pages 30 and 31 of this edition.

Attributes which are expected in a Party member in a leading position :
Appointments to leading positions shall only be made when the Party member shows by his personal and social life that he is worthy.
Is not servile to those in authority.
Does not give himself airs when addressing his juniors.
Who always has the courage to express the absolute truth.
Who is so deeply immersed in his work that he cannot be deflected from the path of duty.

Especially must leading Party members ensure that they are able :
To be able to decide between right and wrong, between Justice and Injustice.
To practise self-control.
To lay their plans with consideration and judgement.
To do their work thoroughly.
To remain loyal to their given word.
Never to promise that which they cannot fulfil.
To be direct.
To win the love and respect of others by their example.

The Oath taken by Political Leaders

Political Leaders take the Oath of Allegiance, annually. The text of the Oath is as follows :

'I swear absolute loyalty to Adolf Hitler. I swear to him and to the leaders whom he sets in authority over me, unconditional obedience.'

Political Leaders must feel that they are inseparable from the principles and the organization of the National Socialist Workers' Party. The oath which is taken can only be broken by death or if the oath-taker is expelled from the National Socialist community.

The protection of Political Leaders against defamatory attacks

The law against malicious attacks upon the State and the Party protects the leading personalities of the State and the Party against defamatory attacks.

This law protects, mainly, leading Party members above the rank of Gauleiter.

Should any accusation arise which could reduce the Party's authority or that of its organizations (eg, the assertion that a Kreisleiter has misappropriated funds and that nothing is being done about it; that is to say, that criminal acts are being tolerated), then proceedings shall be taken under Paragraph 1 of the law.

Where such attacks defame the Party and its officers, consultation with the judicial office of the Party shall decide whether to lay this information before the appropriate legal authorities.

Relations with those superior in rank

A difference in rank does not always imply a superiority in ranks. An incumbent is, for example, senior to all Political Leaders within his area and has absolute administrative authority over them. But he is not the superior officer of Political Leaders of other administrative areas.

The same applies to the office of Section Leader (Amtsleiter). A chain of command is to be maintained in respect of those junior in rank.

In cases of emergency Political Leaders can be ordered, by the incumbent, or by a Section Leader (Amtsleiter), from the rank of Local Group Leader (Ortsgruppenleiter) or Kreisamtsleiter upwards, including Main Section Leader (Hauptstellenleiter) at national level, to take up a temporary appointment.

Where a Political Leader has to appear in public, or is kept in the public eye, all those Political Leaders who are his superiors are not only empowered but are required to take the necessary action.

The paying of compliments by stationary or marching groups of Political Leaders

When bodies of Political Leaders are on parade, either stationary or on the march, only the Political Leader commanding the detachment shall give the German salute.

When the Horst Wessel song or *Deutschland über Alles* are being sung only the Political Leader commanding the detachment shall raise his right arm in the German salute. Upon the word of command 'Attention', all other Political Leaders within the formation shall stand still without raising their arms.

This does not apply to Political Leaders who do not form part of an organized body. In such cases the individual shall raise his right arm.

Inside a building Political Leaders, members of organizations or associations appearing in uniform, and not carrying out duties as escorts to the Colour, inner or outer line of sentries, etc, shall, upon entry of the Colours into the hall or upon the singing of the National Anthem, salute in the German fashion but with heads bared.

The same applies to those appearing in civilian clothes.

At open-air ceremonies the German greeting shall be given, by those in uniform, with covered heads. Those in civilian clothes remove their headdress.

Designation and Appointment

A distinction is made between Designation and Appointment. Designations are made within an administrative area. Appointments are made in regard to rank. Thus a Party member can be designated by a Gauleiter to take up the post of a Regional Press Officer (Gaupresseamtsleiter), etc. This does not necessarily imply that the corresponding rank is automatically granted. In examples like that given above this can only be given by the Führer.

Designations, dismissals and postings of Political Leaders by the appropriate incumbent shall only be made after prior discussion with the next senior office of the Political Leader under discussion.

Designations of Political Leaders

Designation to an office is an indication of the trust placed in a Party member to lead one of the Party's sections. This should only be carried out after interview and a probationary period has shown the Party member's fitness to hold the office. Designation does not imply the granting of rank.

Designations are made by:

(a) Reichsleiter for all offices within the National leadership subordinate to them: by senior members of the Party judiciary, or the Party Treasurer's Department, and the Leader of the German Workers' Front, after contact has been made with the appropriate Gauleiter, in respect of Regional judiciary members, regional treasurers and regional foremen of the German Workers' Front.

(b) Leaders of Ministries or Departments within the National leadership, within their area of authority and after informing the Head of the National Organization Department.

(c) Regional Leaders, District Leaders, Local Group Leaders for posts within their spheres of influence. By Leaders of Departments within the provinces of the incumbents named above, for all posts below their grade and with the agreement of the appropriate incumbent.

Designation of Party members to offices within the National leadership, as well as the designation of Deputy Regional Leaders and others to the level of District Leaders, is to be reported immediately to the Head of the National Organization Department of the NSDAP.

A Party member who is designated, for the first time, to take up a Party office must prove his capabilities for holding the office by undergoing a probationary period of not less than three months.

During this period he has to produce his family tree, if this has not already been done, going back to the year 1800.

The requirement to produce proof of racial purity where the family tree is incomplete follows the instructions laid down by the Personnel Department of the NSDAP.

Where personal files already exist in the Personnel Department in respect of a Political Leader, then upon his being designated in some other office, a new file is not to be opened but the old ones brought up to date.

The Designee shall sign m.d.L.b. (mit der Leitung beauftragt), ie, 'empowered with the office of'.

Where suspensions from office occur as a result of the demand of the Party Court, designation of a successor shall be put off until the decision of the Court is made known. The duties of the suspended member shall, in such cases, be carried out by a Political Leader already carrying out the task.

The Party member entrusted with these duties shall sign himself m.d.W.d.G.b. (mit der Wahrnehmung der Geschäfte beauftragte), ie, 'entrusted with carrying out the duties'.

Application to be confirmed as a Designee and, therefore, to have a claim to the appropriate rank must be received not later than three months after being designated and must be accompanied by a written communication asking for reasons why the Designee should not be confirmed in his office.

The appointment of Political Leaders

1. The Führer makes appointments of the following Political Leaders:
   (a) Reichsleiter and all Political Leaders, including women's leaders within the National leadership.
   (b) Regional Leaders (Gauleiter) and to Head of a Department at Regional level, including the women's regional organization.
   (c) District Leaders (Kreisleiter).
   These appointments are printed in the official gazette.

2. Regional Leaders' name:
   (a) Political Leaders, including those in the women's organization, at Regional level, that is the Heads of Main Sections and Assistants.
   (b) Political Leaders, including those in the women's organization, at District (Kreis) level.
   (c) Local Group Leaders (Ortsgruppenleiter)

3. District Leaders' name:
   Political Leaders, including those in the women's organization, at Local

Group level, including Block and Cell Leaders, Block Assistants as well as the Political Leaders in factories (as long as these are Party members). All Political Leaders, including those in the women's organization, receive proof of identity.

The rating of Political Leaders

In order to qualify for rating within the organization of Political Leaders, written authority must be obtained.

For Reichsleiter and Gauleiter (Regional Leaders) this authority is granted by the Führer. For Political Leaders at National level by the Party Chancery, and for District Leaders (Kreisleiter), Local Group Leaders (Ortsgruppenleiter) and Political Leaders at regional, district or local level, by the Regional Leader (Gauleiter).

Suspensions

The temporary suspension of a Political Leader is to be announced by the same authority which designated him. The responsible office are to report the suspension of a Political Leader to the appropriate Personnel Office.

Dismissals

The dismissal of a Political Leader is to be announced by the same authority which appointed him.

The proposal to dismiss a Political Leader is to be stated in writing.

A Political Leader cannot lay down his office upon his own authority. Such an act would be considered to be dereliction of duty. A Political Leader can only apply to his superior for permission to resign his office.

Deputization

With the one exception of 'Deputy Regional Leader' (Stellvertretende Gauleiter), there is no other office within the Party or within its associate organizations where the term 'Deputy' is to be used. It is, therefore, forbidden to use such description as Deputy District Leader, Deputy Regional Departmental Head or the like. (The exceptions to this rule are those covered by the terms of the German Workers' Front Leipzig Agreement of 21 March 1935.)

Every incumbent should, from time to time, entrust, when required, the running of his office to an Assistant. This person is, however, never to be described as a Deputy.

Seconding

It is necessary that qualified Political Leaders should, on occasion, be seconded to the next highest office. Thus, suitable Block Leaders or Cell Leaders should be brought onto the staff of the Local Group; suitably qualified Local Group Leaders be seconded to area staffs and Area Leaders (Kreisleiter) taken, temporarily, onto Regional staffs or even to staffs at National level, so long as this can be done without harm to their own department. The Head of the National Organization Department and his subordinate Personnel Departments are responsible for carrying out such secondings.

Personal Documents for Political Leaders

These are: Identity card with photograph.
Table showing Aryan descent.

Candidates for Leadership in Ordensburg schools or Adolf Hitler pupils have, in addition to the above documents, to produce a table of racial purity and a chart of his family antecedents (Sippentafel).

The forms to be used are those supplied by the Personnel Department of the Head of the National Organization of the NSDAP. These forms are obtainable from the National Administration Department of the Treasurer's Department.

Applications for Appointments, Suspensions, Postings and Dismissals on behalf of Political Leaders in Party offices shall be made by the Head of the appropriate section to the appropriate Personnel Department responsible for carrying out action on these applications.

Applications for Appointments, Suspensions, Postings and Dismissals on behalf of Political Leaders, administrators and members of the women's organizations or their associate bodies shall be sent to the Personnel Department of those organizations for onward transmission to the appropriate Personnel Department for their action.

The return of identity documents signed by the incumbent shall be carried out in the same fashion.

Uniforms, badges of rank and insignia of office worn by Political Leaders of the NSDAP

I. Political Leaders' uniforms

A. General information regarding the wearing of Uniform

The Political Leaders' uniform came into being out of the recognition that the basis of political work for Germany is military.

By instituting this the Führer has visibly expressed his intention to draw a clear distinction between the type of person who is a Political Leader of the NSDAP and the civil politicians of former Parties and States.

The Political Leader is a Preacher and a Soldier at one and the same time; he represents that type of political leadership for which the German people has struggled for two thousand years.

The Political Leader must be conscious of this high mission when he wears the uniform of honour which the Führer has awarded him.

All Political Leaders, irrespective of which Local Group, District, or Region of Germany in which they serve, wear a standard uniform.

All Political Leaders, irrespective of their position within the Party whether in the political leadership, administration, the Party Courts, in associated organizations or in factories, wear a standard uniform.

This regulation accords with the National Socialist principle of fellowship, of the equality not only in responsibility but also of the person of all those comrades who are working for the Party.

Local Group Leaders (Ortsgruppenleiter) of the NSDAP and the Political Leaders from Leader of a District Office, of a Regional Main Office or a National Department upwards, also wear, in addition to their brown uniform, a white uniform jacket, ceremonial dress with a brown or white jacket, white walking out dress and the brown double-breasted walking out dress, as well as parade dress with a brown or white jacket.

Not every Political Leader is authorized to wear all the listed uniforms because the NSDAP wishes to avoid the situation that financially prosperous Political Leaders are able to appear better clad than those financially less well off.

Political Leaders are to appear in absolutely correct uniform.

If a correct uniform is not available then civilian clothes are to be worn. A mixture of civilian clothes and uniform is not permitted.

The wearing of Political Leaders' uniform is restricted to those who have

16

Standarte des Führers

Hoheitsfahnen der NSDAP.

München

Kreis

Fahne der Alten Garde der NSDAP.

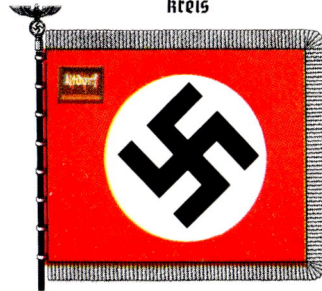

Ortsgruppe

NSDAP Party Colours
TOP LEFT: Führer's Standard.
UPPER LEFT: The Banner of the
Old Guard; the Golden Badge of Honour
of the NSDAP on a red ground.
TOP RIGHT: Area Banner for a Kreis,
with area name.
ABOVE, RIGHT: Area Banner for a
Local Group (Ortsgruppe) with
group name.

proper written authority signed by a responsible officer of his administrative level. Party members who are not Political Leaders are not allowed to wear Political Leaders' uniform (or parts of such uniform) even without badges.

When appearing in formation the dress ordered to be worn shall be that which ensures that the unit, at least in its sub-sections, is uniformly clad.

Political Leaders in uniform shall not smoke in the open streets.

It is not permitted to wear civil decorations or badges of organizations and associations upon the uniform.

Black Crêpe is not to be worn on the Uniform

Regarding the wearing of mourning crêpe on the uniform, the following instructions have been issued:

Where, at funerals or memorial services detached units, or individual Political Leaders, members of organizations and of their associated societies take part in uniform, no mourning crêpe shall be worn.

B. List of Uniforms

1. Service Dress
  (a) Service dress with brown shirt.
  (b) Service dress with light brown jacket.
  (c) Service dress with white jacket.
2. Ceremonial Dress
  (a) Ceremonial dress with light brown jacket.
  (b) Ceremonial dress with white jacket.
3. Parade Dress
  (a) Parade dress with light brown jacket.
  (b) Parade dress with white jacket.
4. Walking Out Dress
  (a) Walking out dress, single-breasted, with light brown jacket (or white jacket).
  (b) Walking out dress, single-breasted, white.
  (c) Walking out dress with double-breasted, light brown or white jacket.
5. Office Dress
  (a) Office dress with service jacket.
  (b) Office dress with white jacket: linen.
  (c) Office dress with brown jacket: twill.

In addition there are uniforms for candidate Political Leaders.

Details of Service Clothing
1. Uniforms
Dress 1a: Service Dress with brown shirt

This dress is authorized to be worn by the following: The standard dress with brown shirt is to be worn by all Political Leaders.

Classification

Cap: Political Leader's cap in light brown tricot, Armed Forces style, with a rust-brown, velvet band and with a fibre peak. Gold cord, gold coloured national emblem, gold coloured oak leaves (embroidered or in metal) and swastika cockade.

Piping in the colour of the level of leadership.

Blouse: Gabardine or twill, light brown, with gold coloured buttons decorated with the national emblem, 24mm diameter for the central buttons and 20mm for the breast pockets.

Piping on the collar patch and collar corresponding to the level of leadership.

Rank Insignia: That of the rank carried.

Party Awards: The Party badge, or the large Golden Badge of Honour, to be worn on the left breast pocket, immediately below the pocket flap, above all other orders and decorations. As a general rule only medal ribbons to be worn.

Armband: Swastika armband showing rank insignia to be worn on the upper left arm.

Tie: Light brown.

Waist Belt: Light Havana brown, leather, 60mm wide, with circular buckle. Under the overcoat a cloth belt of the same colour as that of the waist belt to be worn. (The waist belt to be worn outside the overcoat.)

Pistol: A Walther PPK, calibre 7·65mm (where issued), light Havana brown holster decorated with a gold coloured national emblem, on light Havana brown supporting straps, 35mm wide, and fitted with gold coloured clips.

Gloves: Dark brown buckskin or tricot.

Trousers: Breeches, light brown, in tricot or gabardine.

Footwear: Black, high jackboots, with chisel toes and no toe cap.

Overcoat: Double-breasted, mid-brown, light brown collar and lapels of uniform material (tricot).

Piping on collar patch and collar corresponding to the swastika armband, showing rank insignia, worn on the upper left arm.

Pistol support strap and waist belt buckled outside the greatcoat.

Rank insignia of the rank carried.

The brown shirt to be worn with a cloth belt underneath the overcoat.

The overcoat to be worn buttoned to the neck so that insignia of rank does not show.

Cloak: Brown with golden clasp.

This dress is authorized to be worn by:

At Local level (Ortsgruppe)	The Local Group Leader.
At District level (Kreisleitung)	Political Leaders higher in rank than Head of a Department (Amtsleiter).
At Regional level (Gauleitung)	Political Leaders higher in rank than Head of a Main Department (Hauptselleleiter).
At National level (Reichsleitung)	Political Leaders higher in rank than Head of a Department (Stelleleiter).

When appearing with an organised body cloaks shall not be worn.

Dress 1b: Service Dress with light brown jacket

This dress is authorized to be worn by the following: The standard dress of Political Leaders, with the light brown jacket, is to be worn by all Political Leaders.

Classification

Amendments to the uniform dress 1a, are:

Jacket: In tricot or gabardine, light brown, single breasted with patch pockets.

Shirt: White with white, semi-stiff turn-down collar (brown shirt only on special instructions). continued on page 22

Service Dress 1a

With brown shirt
(Oberhelfer)

With overcoat
(Helfer)

Service Dress

1b: With brown jacket
(Bereitschaftsleiter)

1c: With white jacket
(Gemeinschaftsleiter)

Ceremonial Dress No 2 with Overcoat
(Haupt-
Gemeinschaftsleiter)

(Abschnittsleiter)

Ceremonial Dress

2a: With brown jacket
(Haupt-
Abschnittsleiter)

2b: With white jacket
(Gemeinschaftsleiter)

Ceremonial Dress

Spielmannszugführer (drum major)
of Gauleitung

Spielmann (drummer)
of Gauleitung

21

Overcoat: The top three buttons to be left open. When marching in an organized body the overcoat to be worn closed. At District level the Kreisleiter and at Regional and National level, Political Leaders above the rank of Head of a Department (Amtsleiter) are permitted to leave open the top three buttons of the overcoat, so long as they are marching at the head of an organized body.

Cloak: Those authorized to wear one; as in Dress 1a.

Dress 1c: Service Dress with white jacket

This dress is authorized to be worn by the following:

At Local level (Ortsgruppe)	The Local Group Leader.
At District level (Kreisleitung)	Political Leaders higher in rank than Head of a Department (Amtsleiter).
At Regional level (Gauleitung)	Political Leaders higher in rank than Head of a Main Department (Hauptstellenleiter).
At National level (Reichsleitung)	Political Leaders higher in rank than Head of a Department (Stellenleiter).

The standard dress with white jacket can be worn in summer in place of the light brown jacket, **but not when on parade in an organised body.**

Classification

Variants to the uniform 1a, are:

Cap: White (on the white crown no coloured piping) or light brown.

Jacket: White, wool, gabardine or drill, single-breasted with patch pockets. No piping round the collar.

Shirt: White, with white, semi-stiff turn-down collar.

Gloves: White.

When wearing the white jacket no belt to be worn and no pistol to be carried.

Overcoat: With the white jacket to the service dress, no overcoat to be worn.

Cloak: Those authorized to wear one, as for Dress 1a.

2. Ceremonial Dress
Uniform 2a: Ceremonial Dress with light brown jacket

This dress is authorized to be worn by the following:

At Local Group level (Ortsgruppe)	The Local Group Leader.
At District level (Kreisleitung)	Political Leaders higher in rank than Head of a Department (Leiter eines Amtes).
At Regional level (Gauleitung)	Political Leaders higher in rank than Head of a Main Department (Hauptstellenleiter).
At National level (Reichsleitung)	Political Leaders higher in rank than Head of a Department (Leiter einer Stelle).

Ceremonial dress shall be worn at all ceremonial, official occasions involving the Party, its organizations and associate groups, the Armed Services, the State, etc, or upon any functions when Political Leaders appear as Guests of Honour.

Other Political Leaders at functions named above shall wear the uniform 1b with a white shirt and a white, semi-stiff, turn-down collar.

Classification

Cap: Light brown. The piping worn shall be that authorized for the level of leadership.

Jacket: Of tricot or gabardine, light brown with patch pockets, single-breasted. Piping on the collar patch and on the collar shall be that colour authorized for the level of leadership.

Rank Insignia: That of the rank carried.

Party Awards: The Party badge or the large Golden Decorations of Honour worn on the left breast pocket, immediately below the pocket flap, above all other orders and decorations.

Medal ribbons only unless the wearing of a full set is ordered.

Armband: Swastika armband showing rank insignia.

Shirt: White, with white turn-down collar.

Tie: Light brown.

Waist Belt, Full Dress: Gold coloured, woven, with dark brown underlay, 52mm wide.

Pistol: Holster in light Havana brown, lacquered on a gold coloured woven supporting strap, 40mm wide.

Gloves: White, buckskin or tricot.

Trousers: Breeches, light brown.

Boots: Black, high.

Overcoat: Piping on the collar patch and on the collar corresponding to the level of leadership.

Swastika armband with rank insignia.

Waist belt and pistol supporting straps (gold coloured, woven) worn outside the overcoat. Lacquered pistol holster.

Rank insignia that of the rank carried.

The top three buttons of the overcoat are to be left unfastened.

Cloak: Those authorized to wear this are shown in Uniform 1a.

Uniform 2b: Ceremonial Dress with the white jacket

This dress is authorized to be worn by the following: those authorized to wear Uniform 2a.

The ceremonial dress with white jacket can be worn in summer at all ceremonial, official occasions involving the Party, its organizations and associate groups, the Armed Forces, the State, etc, or on other occasions when Political Leaders appear as Guests of Honour; but it is not to be worn when on parade with an organized body.

Classification

Variants to Uniform 2a, are:

Cap: With white or light brown crown.

Jacket: White, wool, gabardine or sail cloth, single-breasted, with patch pockets.

Waist Belt, Full Dress: White, underlaid.

Pistol Support Straps: Gold coloured, woven, with lacquered holster.

Overcoat: No overcoat shall be worn with a ceremonial uniform white jacket.

Cloak: As for Uniform 1a.

continued on page 26

Walking Out Dress

4a : With brown jacket
    (Haupt-
Bereitschaftsleiter)

4c : With DB jacket
    (Dienstleiter)

Walking Out Dress

4b : White dress
    (Bereichsleiter)

4d : White jacket
    (Bereichsleiter)

Walking Out Dress
With overcoat
(Ober-befehlsleiter)

Walking Out Dress
With cape

24

Office Dress

5a : With brown jacket
(Oberarbeitsleiter)

5b : With white jacket
(Einsatzleiter)

**Political Leader
Candidate**
Service Dress 1b

**Ordensburg
Commanding Officer**
Service Dress 1b
(Gemeinschaftseiter)

RIGHT: Dr. Robert Ley in the service dress of a Reichsleiter, worn here without cap or belt on an informal factory tour. He wears the Imperial German Air Observer badge at the bottom right of his breast pocket. Following him is a Gauleiter in service dress.

3. Parade Dress

Uniform 3a: Parade Dress with light brown jacket

This dress is authorized to be worn by the following:

At Local Group level (Ortsgruppe)	The Local Group Leader.
At District level (Kreisleitung)	Political Leaders higher in rank than Head of a Department (Leiter eines Amtes).
At Regional level (Gauleitung)	Political Leaders higher in rank than Head of a Main Department (Hauptstellenleiter).
At National level (Reichsleitung)	Political Leaders higher in rank than Head of a Department (Leiter einer Stelle).

Parade dress with a light brown jacket shall be worn upon special ceremonial occasions and only when ordered.

Uniform 3b: Parade Dress with white jacket

This dress is authorized to be worn by the following: those mentioned for Uniform 3a.

Parade dress with a white jacket shall be worn upon special ceremonial occasions and only when ordered.

4. Walking Out Dress

Uniform 4a: Walking Out Dress, single-breasted, light brown

This dress is authorized to be worn by the following: walking out dress, single-breasted, light brown, can be worn by all Political Leaders.

Classification

Cap: Light brown, the piping worn shall be in the colour of the level of leadership.

Jacket: Tricot or gabardine, light brown with slit pockets, single-breasted (it is permitted to wear patch pockets). Piping on the collar patch and on the collar in the colour of the level of leadership.

A single-breasted white jacket can be worn in place of the single-breasted light brown jacket.

Those authorized to wear the white jacket:

At Local Group level (Ortsgruppe)	The Local Group Leader.
At District level (Kreisleitung)	Political Leaders higher in rank than Head of a Department (Leiter eines Amtes).
At Regional level (Gauleitung)	Political Leaders higher in rank than Head of a Main Department (Haupstellenleiter).
At National level (Reichsleitung)	Political Leaders higher in rank than Head of a Department (Leiter einer Stelle).

Rank Insignia: That of the rank carried.

Party Awards: Party badge or the large Golden Decoration of Honour worn on the left breast pocket below the pocket flap above all other orders and decorations. Medal ribbons (on special festive occasions full set of medals).

Armband: Swastika armband with rank insignia.
Shirt: White with turn-down collar.

Uniform 4b: Walking Out Dress, single-breasted, white

This dress is authorized to be worn by the following:

At Local level (Ortsgruppe)	The Local Group Leader.
At District level (Kreisleitung)	Political Leaders higher in rank than Head of a Department (Leiter eines Amtes).
At Regional level (Gauleitung)	Political Leaders higher in rank than Head of a Main Department (Hauptstellenleiter).
At National level (Reichsleitung)	Political Leaders higher in rank than Head of a Department (Leiter einer Stelle).

The single-breasted, white, walking out dress can be worn out of doors, in summer, under suitable weather conditions.

Classification

Variants to Uniform 4a, are:
Cap: With white crown only.
Jacket: White, wool gabardine or sail cloth, single-breasted with slit pockets (patch pockets can also be worn on the white jacket).
Trousers: Long, white.
Shoes: White, linen shoes with brown sole and heel, white socks.
Gloves: White.

When wearing the walking out dress of single-breasted white jacket and long, white trousers is worn, no overcoat, no cloak, no ceremonial belt or waist belt are to be worn, nor is a pistol to be carried. This dress can, therefore, only be worn upon those occasions where an overcoat or cloak are not required.

Uniform 4c: Walking Out Dress, double-breasted, light brown or white

This dress is authorized to be worn by the following:

At Local level (Ortsgruppe)	The Local Group Leader.
At District level (Kreisleitung)	Political Leaders higher in rank than Head of a Department (Leiter eines Amtes).
At Regional level (Gauleitung)	Political Leaders higher in rank than Head of a Main Department (Hauptstellenleiter).
At National level (Reichsleitung)	Political Leaders higher in rank than Head of a Department (Stellenleiter).

Classification

Variants to Uniform 4a, are:
Jacket: Double-breasted, light brown tricot or gabardine, with slit side pockets or a jacket, double-breasted, white without ceremonial belt.

Party badge or the large Golden Badge of Honour on the left breast pocket.

An overcoat with ceremonial belt or a cloak is worn with the brown jacket of the double-breasted walking out dress. continued on page 30

27

Dienstftellungsabzeichen auf der Armbinde
der Politifchen Leiter der NSDAP. in der Gauleitung

Armbands for Gauleitung personnel. Compare with detail listings and patterns starting on page 43.

Kraftwagenftander in der Gauleitung

Gauleiter

Stellvertretender Gauleiter

Leiter eines Haupt- amtes

Motor-car pennants for Gauleitung personnel.

Leiter eines Amtes

Gaufrauenfchaftsleiterin

Dienftrangabzeichen der Politifchen Leiter der NSDAP.
in der Gauleitung

Collar patch rank insignia for Gauleitung personnel.

Abzeichen für Frauenfchaftsleiterinnen

Lower row of badges apply to the Women's League of the NSDAP which is not covered in the text.

Dienſtſtellungsabzeichen auf der Armbinde der Politiſchen Leiter der NSDAP. in der Ortsgruppe

Armbands for Ortsgruppe personnel. Compare with detail listings and patterns starting on page 43.

Kraftwagenſtander in der Ortsgruppe

Motor-car pennant for Ortsgruppenleiter.

Collar patch rank insignia for Ortsgruppe personnel.

Dienſtrangabzeichen der Politiſchen Leiter der NSDAP. in der Ortsgruppe

Abzeichen für Frauenſchaftsleiterinnen

Lower row of badges apply to the Women's League of the NSDAP which is not covered in the text.

No overcoat is worn with the double-breasted walking out dress with white jacket. A cloak is worn in its place.

5. Office Dress

This dress is authorized to be worn by the following: Political Leaders' Office Dress can be worn by all those working in offices on behalf of the Party, its branches (The National Socialist Students' League, National Socialist Academic Officers' League) and associate organizations including those working at Local Group level and Local Group administration level in senior positions and by honorary Political Leaders.

There are three types of office dress, and these are:

Office Dress: (a) With light brown uniform jacket.
　　　　　　　(b) With white linen jacket.
　　　　　　　(c) With light brown twill jacket.

Classification

Uniform 5a: Office Dress with light brown uniform jacket

Jacket: Tricot or gabardine, single-breasted.

Buttons: Gold coloured and bearing the national emblem.

Patch or slit pockets.

Piping on collar patch and collar in the colour of the level of leadership.

Rank insignia that of the rank carried.

Party badge or the large Golden Badge of Honour on the left breast pocket, immediately below the pocket flap.

No medals.

Uniform 5b: Office Dress with white linen jacket

Other variants as for 5a.

Uniform 5c: Office Dress with twill jacket

Light brown twill.

Other variants as for 1a.

With Office Dress the following are worn:

Armband: Swastika armband showing rank insignia to be worn on left upper arm.

Shirt: Brown shirt with turn-down collar or a white shirt.

Tie: Light brown.

Trousers: Long, dark brown of uniform material with light brown braiding, but without turn-ups and without a strap.

Socks: Black.

Shoes: Black.

Gloves: Dark brown buckskin or tricot.

In the street only office dress with the light brown jacket shall be worn unless covered by an overcoat or cloak (in both cases with a waist belt). A pistol is not worn when wearing office dress (even with the overcoat).

Cloak: Those authorized to wear this as Uniform 1a.

Uniform for Political Leader Candidates

Those Party members who are selected, for the first time, to serve in a Section, Department, a Main Department or a Cell, and for whom the position is being kept open until they can become Political Leaders at the end of a three-month probationary period, can receive permission to wear the uniform of a Political Leader Candidate.

The Candidate Political Leader's uniform is that of the Political Leader.

The Candidate Political Leader can wear:

    Uniform 1a: The uniform with blouse

    Uniform 1a: The uniform with light brown jacket

or upon special occasions:

    Uniform 4a: Walking Out Dress, light brown, single-breasted

                 and

    Uniform 5: Office Dress,

with an armband bearing no rank insignia but with piping of the level of leadership.

If the Candidate Political Leader is not a Party member, the collar patches on his tunic bear neither the national emblem nor rank insginia.

For Candidate Political Leaders the collar patch, as well as the piping surrounding this, is to be that of the level of leadership.

Candidate Political Leaders are not authorized to wear a pistol.

Summer Overcoats for Political Leaders

Summer overcoats made of a light, waterproof material of the same colour and having the same cut as the uniform overcoat may be worn by Political Leaders.

LEFT: Reichsleiter Franz von Epp in white service dress jacket (Uniform 1c). ABOVE, LEFT: Reichsleiter Franz von Epp in walking out dress with overcoat (Uniform 4a). Note distinctive gold braid on the Reichsleiter armband. A member of the AO (Auslands Organisation) which had the status of a Gau. Note AO diamond on lower left sleeve.

Collar patch rank badges
for Reichsleitung personnel.
Compare with detail
listings and patterns
on page 43.

Dienſtrangabzeichen der Politiſchen Leiter der NSDAP.
in der Reichsleitung

Politiſcher Leiter-Anwärter (Pg.) · Politiſcher Leiter-Anwärter (Nicht-Pg.) · Helfer · Oberhelfer

Arbeitsleiter · Ober-Arbeitsleiter · Haupt-Arbeitsleiter · Abſchnittsleiter · Ober-Abſchnittsleiter · Haupt-Abſchnittsleiter

Bereitſchaftsleiter · Ober-Bereitſchaftsleiter · Haupt-Bereitſchaftsleiter · Bereichsleiter · Ober-Bereichsleiter · Haupt-Bereichsleiter

Einſatzleiter · Ober-Einſatzleiter · Haupt-Einſatzleiter · Dienſtleiter · Ober-Dienſtleiter · Haupt-Dienſtleiter

Gemeinſchaftsleiter · Ober-Gemeinſchaftsleiter · Haupt-Gemeinſchaftsleiter · Befehlsleiter · Ober-Befehlsleiter · Haupt-Befehlsleiter

Reichsleiter

Abzeichen für Frauenſchaftsleiterinnen

Sonderbeauftragter der NSDAP. · Reichsfrauenführerin · Engerer Stab · Erweiterter Stab · Sonſtige Mitarbeiterinnen (auch Nicht-Pggn.) · Sämtliche ausgeſchiedenen Mitarbeiterinnen uſw.

Lower row shows badges
for Women's League of
NSDAP, not covered in
this book.

Dienſtſtellungsabzeichen auf der Armbinde
der Politiſchen Leiter der NSDAP. in der Reichsleitung

Politiſcher-Leiter-Anwärter · Sonderbeauftragter: weiße Scheibe u. Hakenkreuz mit golfl. Einfaſſung · Mitarbeiter, Leiter eines Hilfslampebüros, Leiter eines Sachgebietes · Leiter einer Hilfsſtelle

Leiter einer Stelle · Leiter einer Hauptſtelle · Leiter eines Amtes

Leiter eines Hauptamtes · Leiter eines Ob. Amtes · Reichsleiter

Kraftwagenſtander in der Reichsleitung

Reichsleiter · Leiter eines Ob. Amtes, Leiter eines Hauptamtes · Leiter eines Amtes

Leiter einer Hauptſtelle · Reichsfrauenführerin · Hauptabteilungsleiterin

Motor-car pennants; last
two are for Women's
League.

Dienstrangabzeichen der Politischen Leiter der NSDAP. in der Kreisleitung

Politischer-Leiter-Anwärter (Nicht-Pg.)

Politischer-Leiter-Anwärter (Pg.)

Helfer

Oberhelfer

Arbeitsleiter

Ober-Arbeitsleiter

Haupt-Arbeitsleiter

Abschnittsleiter

Ober-Abschnittsleiter

Haupt-Abschnittsleiter

Bereitschaftsleiter

Ober-Bereitschaftsleiter

Haupt-Bereitschaftsleiter

Bereichsleiter

Ober-Bereichsleiter

Haupt-Bereichsleiter

Einsatzleiter

Ober-Einsatzleiter

Haupt-Einsatzleiter

Dienstleiter

Gemeinschaftsleiter

Ober-Gemeinschaftsleiter

Haupt-Gemeinschaftsleiter

Abzeichen für Frauenschaftsleiterinnen

Sonderbeauftragter der NSDAP.

Kreisfrauenschafts-leiterin

Engerer Stab

Erweiterter Stab

Sonstige Mitarbeiterinnen (auch Nicht-Pggn.)

Sämtliche ausgeschiedenen Mitarbeiterinnen usw.

Collar patch rank badges for Kreisleitung personnel. Base colour brown. Lower panel shows badges for specially employed persons and Women's League which are not covered in this book.

33

Dienststellungsabzeichen auf der Armbinde
der Politischen Leiter der NSDAP. in der Kreisleitung

Politischer-Leiter-Anwärter
Sonderbeauftragter: weiße Scheibe
u. hakenkreuz mit goldf. Einfassung

Mitarbeiter,
Leiter eines hilfsfachgebietes,
Leiter eines Sachgebietes

Leiter einer hilfsstelle

Leiter einer Stelle

Leiter einer hauptstelle

Leiter eines Amtes

Leiter eines hauptamtes

Kreisleiter

Kraftwagenstander in der Kreisleitung

Kreisleiter

Leiter eines hauptamtes
Leiter eines Amtes

Kreisfrauenschaftsleiterin

TOP: Armbands for Kreisleitung personnel. BOTTOM: Motor-Car pennants; dark areas are brown.

34

Special sports clothing was designed for NSDAP Political Leaders. The running shoes were black, shorts khaki-brown, singlet white with NSDAP emblem, and track suit dark (navy) blue with white badge.

ABOVE: Dr. Robert Ley (left) in Berlin with Noudenberg, leader of the Dutch Labour Movement. Ley is wearing walking out dress No. 4C which featured the double breasted jacket and dark blue trousers. Shirt is white and tie brown.

**Politische-Leiter-Mütze
in der Ortsgruppe**

**Politische-Leiter-Mütze
im Kreis**

**Politische-Leiter-Mütze
im Gau**

**Politische-Leiter-Mütze
im Reich**

Politische-Leiter-Mütze in Weiß
(Paspel nur am Mützenband)

Leibriemen
60 mm breit

Feldbinde
goldfarben gewirkt

Political leader's caps and belts ; lower belt is the embroidered version for parade wear.

37

TOP: Reichsleiter Walter Funk (left) in double-breasted white walking out dress, with Erich Koch (right), Gauleiter of Ostpreussen. ABOVE: Peaked cap worn by Gemeinschaftsleiter Heinz Franke who was an Amtsleiter (Head of Department) at Kreis level (Imperial War Museum collection).

RIGHT: Dr. Robert Ley, a Reichsleiter, in service dress No. 1A, with overcoat, wearing belt and pistol.

II. Badges of rank and office held by Political Leaders of the NSDAP

A. General information on Badges of Rank and Office

The areas in which Political Leaders work are all-embracing and of the most diverse type.

It was in 1933 that the Führer first gave to the Political Leaders insignia which was, on the one hand, to be a visible recognition of their work and, on the other hand, to be the means of identifying them within the organization.

The result of the expansion of the NSDAP and that of the many years steadfastness in the fulfilment of their duty made it necessary to improve, by careful selection, the badges worn over the years by Political Leaders.

Up to the present time, badges worn by Political Leaders showed both the wearer's rank and area of responsibility. There were no opportunities for promotion once the rank had been bestowed—unless a higher post was included.

These new badges give opportunities for promotion to those Political Leaders, who of necessity have had to spend years, perhaps even decades, in one post, eg, as a Local Group Leader.

The Führer has, therefore, decreed that the new badges for Political Leaders should be separate and should indicate

Rank and Level of Leadership

Rank is shown on the collar patch and the level of leadership by the relevant markings on the armband.

At the same time the Führer has ordered that the same badges of rank are to be used in every area of responsibility.

B. Granting of Rank in the NSDAP

Rank can only be given to the leaders of those posts whose establishment has been approved by the Führer, upon the recommendation of the Head of the National Organization's (Reichsorganisationsleiter) head organizing office.

Oberdeinstleiter Leo Jennes in service dress. Note the collar patches which indicate the rank. The deep turn-back on the cuff was a feature common to the uniforms of other organizations.

C. Plan of the Ranks and Insignia of the NSDAP's Political Leaders

INSIGNIA	RANK	DESCRIPTION
	PL Anwärter (Political Leader Candidate: non-party member)	Without the National Emblem or badges of rank.
	PL Anwärter (Political Leader Candidate: Party member)	National Emblem without badges of rank.
	Helfer (Assistant)	National Emblem with one golden stripe.
	Oberhelfer (Senior Assistant)	National Emblem and two golden stripes.
	Arbeitsleiter (Work Director)	National Emblem and one golden star.
	Ober-Arbeitsleiter (Senior Work Director)	National Emblem with one golden star and one golden stripe.
	Haupt-Arbeitsleiter (Main Work Director)	National Emblem with one golden star and two golden stripes.
	Bereitschaftsleiter	National Emblem and two golden stars.
	Ober-Bereitschaftsleiter	National Emblem with two golden stars and one golden stripe.
	Haupt-Bereitschaftsleiter	National Emblem with two golden stars and two golden stripes.

INSIGNIA	RANK	DESCRIPTION
	Einsatzleiter	National Emblem and three golden stars.
	Ober-Einsatzleiter	National Emblem with three golden stars and one golden stripe.
	Haupt-Einsatzleiter	National Emblem with three golden stars and two golden stripes.
	Gemeinschaftsleiter	National Emblem and four golden stars.
	Ober-Gemeinschaftsleiter	National Emblem with four golden stars and one golden stripe.
	Haupt-Gemeinschaftsleiter	National Emblem with four golden stars and two golden stripes.
	Abschnittsleiter	National Emblem and one golden oak leaf.
	Ober-Abschnittsleiter	National Emblem with one golden oak leaf and one band of lace in oak-leaf pattern.
	Haupt-Abschnittsleiter	National Emblem with one golden oak leaf and two bands of lace in oak-leaf pattern.

Plan of the Ranks and Insignia is continued on next page

INSIGNIA	RANK	DESCRIPTION
	Bereichsleiter	National Emblem and two golden oak leaves.
	Ober-bereichsleiter	National Emblem with two golden oak leaves and one band of lace in oak-leaf pattern.
	Haupt-Bereichsleiter	National Emblem with two golden oak leaves and two bands of lace in oak-leaf pattern.
	Dienstleiter	National Emblem with three golden oak leaves.
	Ober-Dienstleiter	National Emblem with three golden oak leaves and one band of lace in oak-leaf pattern.
	Haupt-Dienstleiter	National Emblem with three golden oak leaves and two bands of lace in oak-leaf pattern.
	Befehlsleiter	National Emblem and four golden oak leaves.
	Ober-Befehlsleiter	National Emblem with four golden oak leaves and one band of lace in oak-leaf pattern.
	Haupt-Befehlsleiter	National Emblem with four golden oak leaves and two bands of lace in oak-leaf pattern.
	Gauleiter	A double row of interwoven, large, golden oak leaves with an embroidered National Emblem in matt gold, in the upper section.
	Reichsleiter	A large, shining gold laurel wreath. Within the wreath a second of matt gold, embroidered oak leaves. Above this a National Emblem.

D. Insignia indicating office held by Political Leaders of the NSDAP

	ARMBAND	DESCRIPTION	WORN BY	ADMINIS-TRATION
1		Without insignia	Political Leader Candidates (Politische Leiter Anwärter)	Factory, mine, etc. Black and Cell, Local Group, Area, Regional and National levels
2		Without insignia but with a golden bordering around the white field and the swastika	Specially employed persons (Sonderbeauftragte)	Area, Regional and National levels
3		With a gold stripe, 1mm wide, at the top and bottom of the armband	Collaborators (Mitarbeiter) Leiter eines Hilfssachgebietes Leiter eines Sachgebietes	Factory, mine, etc. Block and Cell, Local Group Area, Regional and National levels
4		With a strip of gold lace, 3mm wide, at the top and bottom of the armband	Leiter einer Hilfstelle Blockwalter und Blockobmann	As armband No 3 Block
5		With a strip of gold lace of oak-leaf pattern, 7mm wide, at the top and bottom of the armband	Head of a Department (Leiter einer Stelle) Zellenwalter and Zellenobmann	As armband No 3 Cell
6		With a strip of gold lace of oak-leaf pattern, 7mm wide, at the top and bottom of the armband, bordered by a gold stripe 1mm wide	Head of a Main Department Leiter einer Hauptstelle	Local Group Area, Regional and National levels
7		As armband No 5 but with the gold lace borders 16mm wide	Head of a Department (Amtsleiter)	As armband No 6
8		As armband No 6 but with the gold lace borders 16mm wide, and the gold stripe border 1·5mm wide	Head of a Main Department (Leiter eines Hauptamtes)	As armband No 6
9		As armband No 7 but with the gold lace borders 22mm wide	Head of a Senior Department (Leiter eines Ob. Amtes)	National level

D : continued

	ARMBAND	DESCRIPTION	WORN BY	ADMINIS-TRATION
10		With a central strip of gold lace in oak-leaf pattern, 16mm wide, bordered with two gold stripes, each 1mm wide. In the centre of the swastika a gold star. A border of gold stripe, 2mm wide, at the top and bottom of the swastika armband	Ortsgruppenleiter (Local Group Leader)	Ortsgruppe (Local group)
11		As for armband No 6 but with the central strip of gold lace 20mm wide	Kreisleiter (Area Leader)	Kreis (Area)
12		As for armband No 7 but with the gold border to the central strip of lace 3mm in width	Stellvertretender Gauleiter (Deputy Regional Leader)	Gau (Region)
13		As for armband No 8 but with the central strip of gold lace 30mm wide	Gauleiter (Regional Leader)	Gau (Region)
14		At the top and bottom edges of the armband a strip of gold lace, of oak-leaf pattern, each strip being 24mm wide. Each strip bordered by a gold stripe 3mm wide. In the centre of the swastika a gold star	Reichsleiter (Leaders at National level)	Reich (National level)

	ARMBAND	DESCRIPTION	WORN BY	ADMINIS-TRATION
15		With a central gold stripe 3mm wide	Betriebsblockobmann	Factory, workshop, mine, etc.
16		With a central strip of gold lace in oak-leaf pattern, 10mm wide, bordered by a gold stripe 1mm wide. At the top and bottom edge of the armband a border of a 1mm gold stripe	Betriebszellenobmann Hauptbetriebs-zellenobmann	Factory, workshop, mine, etc.
17		With a central gold stripe 3mm wide. With a gold star in the centre of the swastika	Blockhelfer *or* Betriebsobmann (A)	Block Factory, workshop, mine, etc.
18		As for armband No 2 but including a golden star in the centre of the swastika	Blockleiter *or* Betriebsobmann (B)	Block Factory, workshop, mine, etc.
19		With a central strip of gold lace in oak-leaf pattern, 13mm wide, bordered by a gold stripe 1mm wide. At the top and bottom edge of the armband a border of a 1mm gold stripe	Zellenleiter *or* Betriebsobmann (C) Betriebsobmann (D) Hauptbetriebsobmann	Cell *or* Factory

The swastika armband worn by Political Leaders of the NSDAP at Local Group level (including factories) is bordered in a light blue piping, that at District level (Kreisleitung) with white piping; that at Regional level (Gauleitung) with dark red piping and that at National level (Reichsleitung) with golden yellow piping.

The white disc and the black swastika upon the armband is bordered by a golden cord for all Political Leaders with the exception of Candidate Political Leaders.

The oak leaves on the swastika armband point upwards.

1. Political Leaders in the NSDAP Foreign Organization (Auslandsorganization)

Political Leaders who are active in the Foreign Organization of the NSDAP wear below their armband a diamond-shaped square, in black cloth, with the woven or embroidered letters 'AO' in gold, and with a gold edging.

2. Political Leaders who serve in the Party Courts of the NSDAP

Members who are active in courts at District (Kreis) level wear, in addition a brown band on the cuff of their left arm bearing the woven word 'Kreisgericht', and in the highest Party Courts the description 'Oberstes Parteigericht'.

3. Technical officers at Regional (Gau) and District (Kreis) level

Leaders of Regional and District technical offices wear a cuff band on the lower left arm with the inscription of their place of employment.

4. Uniform and insignia indicating level of leadership for specially employed persons

Specially employed persons within the NSDAP wear Political Leader's uniform. On the collar patch a woven oak leaf wreath with a swastika. In addition, a swastika armband without badge. Swastika and the white background framed by a golden cord.

ABOVE: Reichsleiter Dr Alfred Rosenberg. Note piping around his collar on the ceremonial uniform tunic. RIGHT: Reichsleiter Dr Wilhelm Frick in the light brown walking out dress tunic.

ABOVE: The embroidered collar patch is well shown (left) in this picture of Dr Freidrich Rainer, Gauleiter of Kärnten. ABOVE, RIGHT: Obergerichtsleiter Freiherr von Bibra. Collar patches indicate rank. Braid on armband shows him to be a Hauptamtsarbeiter (Head of a Main Office). Note Party badge in standard position on left breast. BELOW, RIGHT: Paul Wegener, Gauleiter of Weser-Ems. Note metal insignia on collar patches. BELOW, LEFT: Gauleiter Erich Koch (East Prussia). Note collar insignia on service dress—brown shirt visible under overcoat.

III. The weapon of honour of a Political Leader (Pistol)

Political Leaders carry as a weapon of honour bestowed by the Führer the pistol (calibre 7·65mm, Walther PPK).

Those authorized to wear the weapon of honour are Political Leaders of the levels of leadership: National, Regional and District level, as well as the Local Group Leader.

In addition, upon the proposal of the responsible officer in the Regional leadership (Gauleitung), Political Leaders at Local Group level can be authorized to wear a pistol. In these cases the Personnel Department of the District (Kreispersonalamt) shall make the appropriate entry into the Political Leader Identity Card of the person concerned.

The pistol is worn fitted to supporting straps, on the right side.

All Political Leaders who carry the Walther PPK pistol must carry out an annual firing practise and be able to produce proof that they can handle the pistol. Responsibility for carrying out shooting practise is the training officer.

Political Leaders take part in competitions whose finals take place during the yearly Party Day Rally.

To obtain, and wear, a fire-arm it is only necessary for incumbents at National, Regional, District and Local Group level, as well as Political Leaders at National, Regional and District level from Head of a Department (Stelleleiter) upwards to produce their Service Identity Card bearing the inscription 'Authorized to wear a fire-arm, calibre 7·65mm'.

Assistants to the rank of Deputy Departmental Heads at National, Regional and District level, as well as Political Leaders at Local Group level require an official Arms Permit and a Certificate of Competence.

IV. Equipment

A. Political Leader's Equipment

(a) Light brown knapsack with sail cloth cover. Fitted with two loops on the waist belt and two carrying straps. These, together with overcoat and mess tin straps, to be in a light Havana brown.

(b) Brown woollen blanket.

(c) Tent, square, in light brown sail cloth.

(d) Mess tin (2-litre) in aluminium, black, burnished, together with knife, fork and spoon.

(e) Drinking cup ($\frac{1}{4}$-litre) in aluminium.

(f) Small pack, light brown (Army pattern).

(g) Water bottle ($\frac{3}{4}$-litre) in aluminium with light brown felt covering and light Havana brown straps.

(h) Overcoat, completely buttoned to the neck (waist belt worn outside).

Wearing of equipment, particularly of the knapsack, is to be ordered for marching only if absolutely required. continued on page 50

OPPOSITE PAGE: Political Leader's pistol, a Walther PPK. The accoutrements shown include standard bearers' gorget plates, aiguilettes for parade wear, and a bandolier for standard bearers, this being of brown material with extensive gold lace. Note the pistol case and belt, this being in polished brown leather with gilt fittings and buckles and NSDAP emblems. PAGE 51: Knapsack (brown) with overcoat and canteen (black). Ration bag (brown canvas) and water-bottle. Bandsmen's 'swallow nests'—Ortsgruppe, light brown and braid; Kreis, dark brown and braid; and Gau, red and braid.

Ehrenwaffe
des Politischen Leiters

Brustschild
für Fahnenträger

Brustschild
für Streifendienst

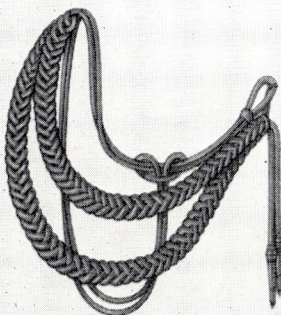

Pistolengehänge
35 mm breit in Leder

2. Ausführung 40 mm breit
goldfarben gewirkt

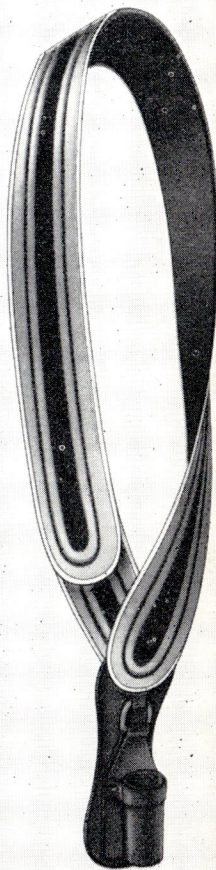

Fangschnur
zum Paradedienstanzug

Bandelier
für Fahnenträger der Kreisleitung
(Ortsgruppe: helleres Braun mit hellblauer Einfaß

B. Ensign's Equipment

Ensigns bearing the Area Banners (Die Hoheitsfahhe) of the NSDAP wear a breast shield, a carrying sash and white gauntlets.

Breast Shield

The National Emblem (Hoheitszeichen) is worn on the old Germanic pattern, burnished breast shield.

Carrying Sash

(a) The Carrying Sash worn by ensigns at Kreis level has a golden fringe covering a dark brown velvet underlay and is piped in white.

(b) At Local Group level the sash of the ensign carrying the Area Banner has a golden fringe with a dark brown velvet underlay and is piped in light blue.

(c) Ensigns bearing DAF Banners wear the same sort of sash as those at Local Group level with white buckskin or tricot gloves, but no breast shield.

C. Musicians' and Bandsmen's Service Dress, Insignia and Equipment

I. Service Dress

1. Service Dress for musicians and bandsmen:
   See Service Dress for Political Leaders (without pistol).
   Drummers have triple shoulder straps in light Havana brown.
2. Walking Out Dress for musicians and bandsmen:
   See Walking Out Dress for Political Leaders.

II. Appointments

Members of Political Leader Bands or Corps of Drums have the following Political Leader appointments:

1. At National Level (Reichs)

(a) The Drum-Major of a Corps of Drums in an Ordensburg school. — Head of a supernumerary office (Hilfsstelle) in a National ministry.

(b) The Drum-Major of a band in an Ordensburg school. — Head of a Departmental Section (Sachgebiet) within a National ministry.

(c) Members of a band or a Corps of Drums in an Oldensburg school. — Assistants in a National ministry.

2. At Regional Level (Gau)

(a) The Drum-Major of a Regional Corps of Drums. — Head of an office in the Regional administration.

Where possible the Regional Inspector of Music should lead the Regional Corps of Drums himself. Only if this is not possible shall the post of Drum-Major of a Regional Corps of Drums be separate from the post of Regional Inspector of Music.

(b) The Drum-Major of the Regional band. — Head of a supernumerary office (Hilfsstelle) in the Regional administration.

(c) Members of a band or Corps of Drums at Regional level. — Assistants in the Regional administration.

3. At District Level (Kreis)

(a) The Drum-Major of a Corps of Drums at District level. — Head of a main office (Hauptstelle) in the District administration.

(b) The Drum-Major of a band at District level. — Head of an office in the District administration.

continued on page 52

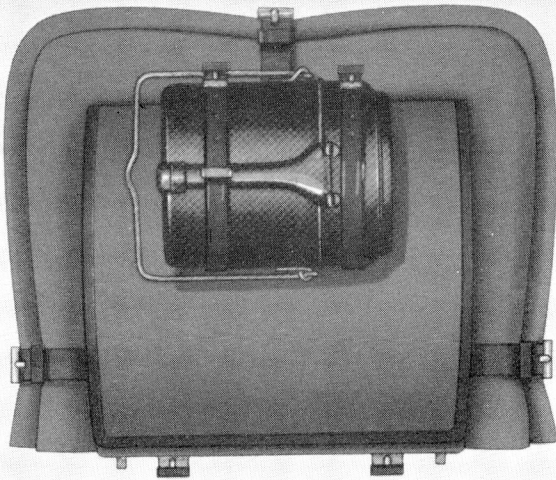

Tornister
mit Decke, Zeltbahn und Kochgeschirr

**Brotbeutel
mit Feldflasche**

**Schwalbennester für Spielmanns-
und Musikzüge**

Spielmannszugführer

Musiker

Spiel-
mann

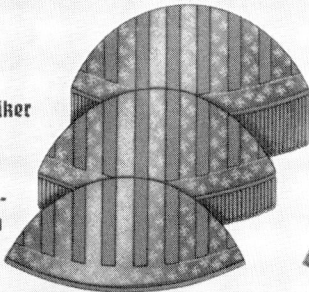

Ortsgruppe   Kreis   Gau

See details on page 48.

(c) Members of a band or Corps of Drums at District level.	From the rank of assistant to that of Head of a supernumerary Departmental Section (Hilfsfachgebiet) in the District administration.

4. At Local Level (Ortsgruppe)

(a) The Drum-Major of a Corps of Drums at Local level.	Head of a main office in the Local administration.
(b) The Drum-Major of a band at Local level.	Head of an office in the Local administration.
(c) Members of a band or Corps of Drums at Local level.	From the rank of assistant to that of Head of a supernumerary Departmental Section (Hilfsfachgebiet) in the Local administration.

5. Factory, Mine or Plant

(a) The Drum-Major of a Corps of Drums within a factory.	Head of an office in the Local administration.
(b) The Drum-Major of a factory band.	Head of a supernumerary office within the Local administration.
(c) Members of a band or Corps of Drums within a factory.	From the rank of assistant to that of Head of a supernumerary Departmental Section of the Local administration.

Members of bands or of Corps of Drums who are not Party members carry patches without the eagle and swastika (Hoheitsabzeichen), that is a patch with the colour and piping of the administrative area to which they belong. In such cases swastika armbands shall not bear insignia and shall not have the border around the swastika or the white background.

A condition of wearing the new badges of rank and insignia on the swastika armband is the possession of a Political Leader's Identity Card correctly endorsed.

III. Musicians' and Bandsmen's Equipment

1. Musicians' Wings (commonly known as 'Swallows' nests')

In addition to rank badges and other insignia, bandsmen and musicians also wear musicians' wings which are issued for all administrative areas. Drum-Majors wear no musicians' wings.

Musicians' wings are issued as follows:

(a) Bandsmen and musicians belonging to bands at Regional level have 'wings' of scarlet cloth and gold coloured lace with interwoven swastikas.

(b) Bandsmen and musicians belonging to bands at District level have 'wings' in dark brown velvet and gold coloured lace with interwoven swastikas.

(c) Bandsmen and musicians belonging to bands at Local level have 'wings' of light brown cloth and gold lace with interwoven swastikas.

Gold coloured fringes are worn on the wings. This is 5cm long for Drum-Majors and 3cms long for musicians.

Bandsmen carry no fringes.

2. The Drum-Major's Staff

The cording and tassels are:

(a) Red-gold for bands at Regional level.

(b) White-gold for bands at District level.

(c) Light blue-gold for bands at Local level.

3. Drums

The drum walls are of brass, decorated round the edges of the walls with triangles of alternate red/white for all bands at Regional, District and Local levels.

4. Fifes

In light Havana brown leather cases.

5. Turkish Musical Crescent (commonly known as a 'Jingling Johnny')

These are only carried by bands at Regional and District level. Red, horse-hair plume. The 'Jingling Johnny' flag, red coloured with gold fringes, and the name of the administrative area in gold coloured Gothic letters. Carrying staff headed by a gold coloured National Emblem.

6. Trumpets

Brass, cords in white-red, trumpet cloth in red with gold fringes. National Emblem, golden, woven on both sides of the trumpet cloth.

7. The Lyra Carillon

Brass, National badge on the head of the carrying staff, gold coloured. The horse-hair plume is coloured:

     (a) Red for bands at Regional level.

     (b) White for bands at District level.

     (c) Light blue for bands at Local level.

Party Colours
Area Banners
(Die Hoheitsfahnen)

The Führer has given to the SA, the SS, the NSKK, the HJ, and the NSD Studentenbund the right to carry unit colours (Sturmfahnen) and to the offices administered by the Party (at Regional, Area and Local level) the right to carry Area Banners (Hoheitsfahnen).

The Area Banner of the Local Group (Ortsgruppe) is the holy symbol of that group.

Party members swear their oath upon the Colour. It is to be lodged in a place of honour in the Local Group offices.

If no such place of honour is available then the Area Leader (Kreisleiter) shall determine its lodging place.

The Area Banner is to be carried only upon Party occasions.

The Local Leader (Ortsgruppenleiter) shall select an available Political Leader and entrust to him the office of standard bearer. Only specially worthy Political Leaders may be selected for this task. Each standard bearer must be imbued with the importance of the office he holds. His watchword is 'The flag still flies even if the standard bearer falls'.

Regulations for the Regional and Area Banners are to be interpreted in the same spirit as those of the Local Group Banner.

The Banner of the Old Guard

This is the symbol of the Old Guard and carries upon its red background the Golden Badge of Honour of the NSDAP. It is carried at the front of the 500 most senior Party Leaders on their annual journey through the German regions.

Flags having a link with Party Tradition

The NS War Victims' Welfare Organization, the Reichbund of German Officials and the NS League of Teachers carry swastika traditional flags. The traditional flags, in respect of the three associate organizations of the Party, are Colours which had been furnished before January 30, 1933 or which, after this date, were procured on behalf of a War Victims' Welfare or Officials group (local group, local administrative group, etc) which had been active on the Party's behalf before the assumption of power.

Dedication of Colours

Swastika banners, DAF banners and Student League banners, etc, can only be dedicated by the Führer or the Provincial Leader (Gauleiter). Such dedications take place ceremonially upon the annual Swearing of the Oath by Political Leaders or upon the occasion of an Area Parade (Kreisappell).

Manufacture of Flags

1. The Swastika Flag (Hoheitsfahne)

The background of woollen naval flag material, scarlet, 140cm long by 120cm broad and edged with silver fringe. On each side is a 90cm diameter circle of white material. Upon this is a swastika in black, standing upon its point, with an arm length of 60cm and an arm width of 12cm.

Patches

Upon the flag's top inside corner is placed a patch, indicating the administrative area which the flag represents. This patch is to be set 5cm from the edge and shall lay horizontally.

(a) *For Regions*—Light red velvet, 16cm high, 21cm wide, edged with a 1cm wide dark red border.

(b) *For Areas (Kreis)*—Red-brown velvet, 16cm high, 21cm wide, edged with a 1cm wide white border.

(c) *For Local Groups (Ortsgruppen)*—Light brown cloth patch, 16cm high, 21cm wide, edged with a 1cm wide light brown cloth.

Within the patch is the name of the Region, Area, etc (but without the description Gau, Kreis or Ortsgruppe).

The letters are embroidered white and Gothic characters.

The Head of the Colour Pike

The National eagle and swastika (Hoheitsadler), silver coloured. Supplied by the National Quartermaster Department (RZM).

2. The Banner of the Student League

The background—On the scarlet background two, horizontal, white parallel lines and upon a white field a standing swastika.

Flag patch—There is on each side of the flag upon its upper, inside corner, a patch 16 × 21cm.

(a) For Student Leaders at Regional level a black patch with the name of the region in white embroidered letters.

(b) For High Schools and Technical School groups a light brown patch with the name of the school (High or Technical) in white letters.

The Head of the Colour Pike

This is in the shape of a spear. Point and ring are chromed.

Student leadership groups at Regional level as well as High School and

Technical School groups consisting of at least 30 members are permitted to carry a banner. Dedication is carried out by the Regional Leader.

Circumstances under which flags may not be carried

It is forbidden for associations and organizations to carry a Party flag which has not been dedicated by the Führer. There are exceptions to this rule and these have special authority.

This prohibition also covers those flags which have a red background with a circular or pointed central white section with any sort of symbol which might, at first glance, be mistaken for a Party ensign (Sturmfahne).

On the other hand, it is allowed for groups, associations and organizations to carry swastika flags so long as these are no larger than 90 × 250cm. This size corresponds to the flag issued by the RZM under the description 'Tragfahne 300'.

It is not permitted to decorate these Colours with special pike heads, patches, decorative nails, embroidery, edgings or streamers.

The Swastika flag 'Tragfahne 300'

Carrying of swastika flags, size 90 × 150cm or smaller, is permitted for associate organizations, societies and school classes.

Flags of this size are described as 'Tragfahne 300' and are obtainable from the RZM or authorized shops.

It is not permitted to decorate these Colours with special pike heads, patches, decorative nails, embroidery, edgings or streamers.

House Flags

The State and National flag (swastika flag) can be flown as a house flag by every German citizen. (The law relating to the flying of flags issued on September 15, 1935.)

There are no regulations regarding the size of house flags.

Marks of Mourning

If detached units of the NSDAP bearing Colours are present at the funeral or at mourning ceremonies, then marks of mourning are to be worn on the flag.

Swastika Arm Bands

The swastika armband is the first symbol of National Socialist solidarity. During the period of struggle it was the visible identification of those who fought actively for the Führer against the mockery and persecution and bloody terror which they encountered whenever they wore this symbol. With this sign they won the fight for Germany. Today the whole German nation seeks to equal the self-sacrifice, the readiness for battle and the attitude of those first National Socialists.

As an eternal reminder of those who paid with their lives for the victory of the swastika, and to awake and to guard the knowledge of their duty to the Führer and his Movement, it is permitted, at Party displays, as well as those of its organizations and associated societies, on State occasions and even for civilian participants to wear the swastika armband.

This permission extends only to organized bodies from factories or workshops, etc, which are part of or members of associate bodies of the Party.

When the meeting is over and the organized bodies have been dismissed from the parade then the swastika armband is to be removed.

Generally speaking those taking part in the parade and who are in uniform are also permitted to wear the armband so long as this does not contravene or conflict with any official or national regulation.

Car Pennants for Political Leaders

The following Political Leaders may fly car pennants:

Nationally	(a) National Leaders (Reichsleiter).
(Reich)	(b) Head of a Ministry or a Main Department.
	(c) Head of a Department.
	(d) Head of a Main Office (Hauptstelle).
Regionally	(a) The Regional Leader (Gauleiter).
(Gau)	(b) Acting Regional Leader.
	(c) Head of a Main Department.
	(d) Head of a Department.
At Area Level	(a) The Area Leader (Kreisleiter).
(Kreis)	(b) Head of a Main Department or of a Department.
At Local Level	The Local Leader (Ortsgruppenleiter).
(Ortsgruppe)	

Pennants are flown on the right side of the vehicle.

On the left side a pennant in the same shape, and similar to a Party flag, shall be flown.

Pennants may only be flown on official journeys made by the incumbent. When the vehicle is being used for non-official journeys, or when the incumbent is not present, the pennant shall be either removed or covered.

Only Political Leaders whose authorization is shown in their Identity Card may fly pennants.

Pennants are issued through the National Quartermaster Department, RZM (Reichszeugmeisterei).

Pennant sizes: (A) 29 × 29cm square, for:

National Leaders (Reichsleiter).

Head of a Ministry or a Main Department at National level.

Head of a Department within the National leadership.

The Regional Leader (Gauleiter).

Acting Regional Leader.

Head of a Main Department at Regional level.

(B) 25 × 40cm, pointed:

Head of a Main Office at National level.

Head of a Department at Regional level.

Leader of a Main Department or Department at Local level.

The pennants are made of embroidered cloth or sheet metal. Details are to be found in coloured Plates 12, 21, 23, 25.*

---

*See pages 28, 29, 32 and 34 in this book.

Decorations of the NSDAP

The official decorations of the Party are:

1. Badges of Honour
1. The Blood Order of November 9, 1923.
2. The Golden Badge of Honour of the NSDAP.
3. The Service Award of the NSDAP.
4. The traditions Regional Award.
5. The Golden Badge of Honour of the Hitler Youth.
6. The Coburg Badge of Honour.
7. The Party Day Badge for Nuremberg, 1929.
8. The Badge for the SA Parade in Braunschweig, 1931.

2. Badges

1. Party Badge.	8. NS Women's League Badge.
2. National Badge.	9. NSVO Badge.
3. The SA Badge.	10. The German Workers' Front Badge.
4. The SS Badge.	11. The National Socialist Welfare Badge.
5. The NSKK Badge.	12. NSKOV Badge.
6. The Students' League Badge.	13. RDB Badge.
7. The Hitler Youth Badge.	14. NSRB Badge.

The Party Badge

Any person who is entitled to a membership card or a membership book of the NSDAP is compelled to wear the Party Badge. In uniform the badge is worn on the left breast pocket. In civilian clothes the Party Badge can be worn in conjunction with the National Emblem of the NSDAP.

RIGHT: Full service dress worn by Fritz Bracht, Gauleiter of Upper Silesia. Note also War Service Cross 2nd class ribbon worn in tunic button in usual position.

Ehrenzeichen der NSDAP.

Goldenes Ehrenzeichen
(kleine Ausführung)

Abzeichen am Band
vom 9. Nov. 1923 (Blutorden)

Goldenes Ehrenzeichen
(große Ausführung)

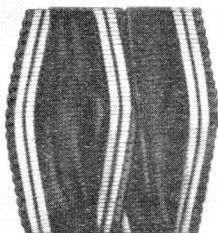

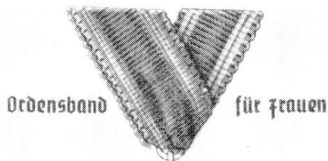

Ordensband   für Frauen

kleine Ordensschnalle

Dienstauszeichnung
(Bronze)

Dienstauszeichnung
(Silber)

Dienstauszeichnung
(Gold)

Tafel 4   Coburger Ehrenzeichen

Reichsparteitag
1929

SA.-Treffen Braunschweig 1931

58

Abzeichen der NSDAP.

Hoheitszeichen
(alte Ausf.)

Partei-Abzeichen

Hoheitszeichen
(neue Ausf.)

SA.-
Abzeichen

SS-
Abzeichen

NSKK.-
Abzeichen

NSFK.-
Abzeichen

HJ.-Abzeichen

Ehrenzeichen
der HJ.

NSD.-Studentenbund
Abzeichen

Ehrenzeichen des
NSD.-Studentenbundes

NSBO.-
Abzeichen

NS.-Frauenschaft
Abzeichen

Deutsches Frauenwerk
Abzeichen

Key to badges in these plates is on next page

The Political Leader and the State

In order to produce the unity of Party and State the leader of the Party Chancery has been empowered with the authority of a National Minister (Reichsminister).

In all fundamental questions the channels of communication between the Ministries and other State authorities and, in reverse, any communication between any State authority with Party organizations, shall go through the Party Chancery. In this fashion the Party and the State viewpoint is in accord.

Appointments to any of these senior posts must be brought to the attention of the Leader of the Party Chancery who will put the Party viewpoint regarding the person of the proposed officer.

To ensure the accord between local government and the Party, the Party representative shall be active in the selection and the dismissing of the Mayor, members of local councils and shall have the decisive voice in the following matters:

1. The decreeing of main clauses.
2. The granting of Freedoms and Honours.

The Head of the Party Chancery shall determine who is the representative of the NSDAP. Upon his instructions the Regional Leader shall name the person. For Town and Area councils the Area Leader (Kreisleiter). Should this person be an official or employee of a local council then an Inspector from the Region is named (Gauinspektor). In special circumstances the Regional Leader (Gauleiter) can name himself as the representative.

Paying Compliments

All Party members whether in civilian clothes or in uniform are to greet each other. In uniform the junior rank greets the senior rank, irrespective of whether the senior rank is a Political Leader, a member of a Party organization, or the

continued on page 62

Decorations of the NSDAP

PAGE 58, LEFT TO RIGHT, TOP TO BOTTOM: Golden Badge of Honour, small (red inner band, gold circle). Blood Order, 9. Nov 1923 (black/white/red/white/ black ribbon, silver medal). Golden Badge of Honour, large. Service Award in bronze (ribbon white stripes on brown). Service Award in silver (light blue/dark blue watered ribbon). Service Award in gold (ribbon white/gold stripes on scarlet, gold emblem). Coburg Badge of Honour (bronze). Party Day Badge, 1929 (gilt). SA-Meeting Braunschweig (white metal). PAGE 59, LEFT TO RIGHT, TOP TO BOTTOM: National emblem, old pattern, Party Badge (red circle), National Badge (later pattern, white metal), SA Badge (silver), SS Badge (black/silver), NSKK Badge (white metal), NSFK, Hitler Youth (red/white), Hitler Youth Honour Badge (red/ white/gold). Students' League Badge (red, black, white), Students' Honour Badge, NSBO Badge, Women's League Arm Badges. OPPOSITE: Special Gau District Badges.

Gau-Ehrenzeichen der NSDAP.

2. Ausführung 1925
**Sachsen, Bayreuth,
Halle-Merseburg, Hessen-
Nassau, Magdeburg-
Anhalt, Mecklenburg**

Berlin
(Gold und Silber)

Ostpreußen
(Silber)

Danzig-Westpreußen
(Silber)
2. Ausführung durchbrochen
und ohne Inschrift

Thüringen
(Silber)

Osthannover
(Gold, Silber, Bronze)

Baden
(Gold und Silber)

Baden
(Silber)

Essen
(Gold und Silber)

Armed Services, etc.

The salute is to the Party and not to the person saluted. It is, therefore, a question of honour. That wearers of the Golden Party Badge are always greeted first is a mark of respect.

Where the ranks are equal the younger person greets the older; but the older must not wait to be greeted. It does no harm if the senior person salutes first. This sometimes has a salutary effect upon the junior ranks.

In cases where there is a doubt as to the question of seniority both sides will salute.

The NSDAP is a comradeship, consequently the Grüssfrage is to be used.

Holders of office (Hoheitstrager) Administrative Areas (Hoheitsgebiete)

Within the ranks of Political Leaders those who hold office occupy a special position. In contrast to the Political Leaders who have professional tasks to occupy them and who are there to advise the office holder, these latter are responsible for what is known as an Administrative Area (Hoheitsgebiet).

Office Holders (Hoheitsträger) are:

The Führer	Local Leaders (Ortsgruppenleiter)
Regional Leaders (Gauleiter)	Cell Leaders (Zellenleiter)
Area Leaders (Kreisleiter)	Block Leaders (Blockleiter)

Administrative Areas are:

The State (Das Reich)	Local Groups (Ortsgruppen)
Regions (Gaue)	Cells (Zellen)
Areas (Kreise)	Blocks (Blocks)

Office holders are entrusted with the political sovereignty of their administrative area. They represent the Party both internally and externally and are responsible for the complete political situation within their area. Incumbents exercise control over the duties of those Party offices under their control and are responsible for the maintenance of discipline within their area. The Heads of Sections, etc, and of associate organizations are, for their part, especially responsible to the incumbent for their spheres of responsibility as well as for their professional offices.

Holders of office are superior to all other Political Leaders in their area. In staff matters incumbents from the rank of Local Leader upwards (Ortsgruppenleiter) have special powers. Within certain limits they can recommend appointments and dismissals of Political Leaders and can have their decisions confirmed by the Party Court of their area.

Party office holders should not be merely administrative officials but should remain in constant touch with the Political Leaders and the people of their administrative area. Incumbents are responsible for the regular and efficient welfare of all the people in their area. At Local level (Ortsgruppe) this must not begin at the administrative offices but should start at Block and Cell level and be carried out by the leaders of those sections. The establishing of regular consultations should give everyone the opportunity of meeting the office holder.

A Local Group (Ortsgruppe) which is constantly engaged upon local

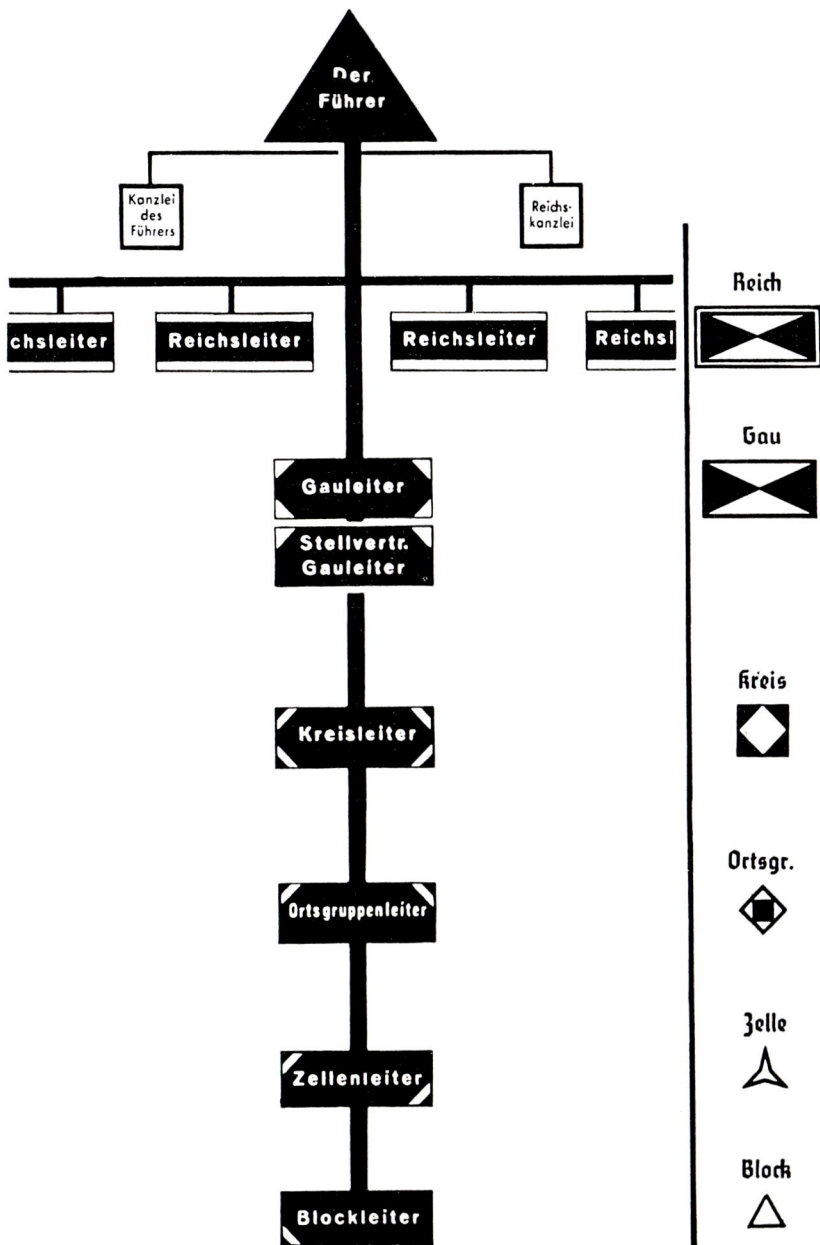

The chain of command from the Führer to Block Leader shown in diagrammatic form. At right are the conventional signs for each grade or office as used in maps, diagram and official documents.

affairs is usually one where the Block and Cell Leaders are not active enough in the right direction and the activities of these leaders must be redirected towards a positive attitude in the task of advising and caring for the welfare of the people they represent.

It is the Party's intention to reach a state where individual members of the public do not contact the Party only in times of trouble, but that the Party, through its own initiative, follows the Führer's directives and studies the well-being of all its people all the time.

Der Jellenleiter der NSDAP.

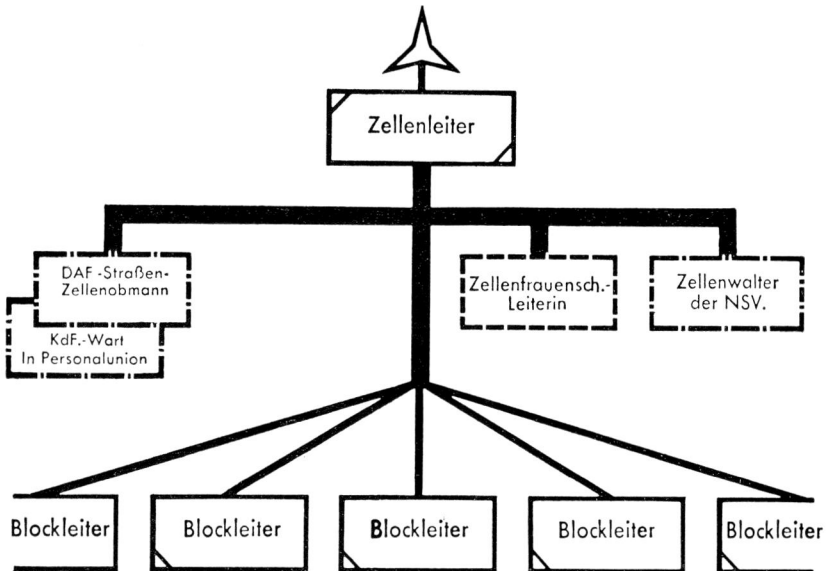

ABOVE: The chain of command between Cell Leader and the Blocks under his supervision. OPPOSITE PAGE, TOP: Block Leader was responsible for a group of units at factory or domestic level. OPPOSITE, LOWER: Conventional signs used in correspondence and documents. See diagram above and on page 63 for examples of the signs in use on the organisation charts reproduced here.

Der Blockleiter der NSDAP.

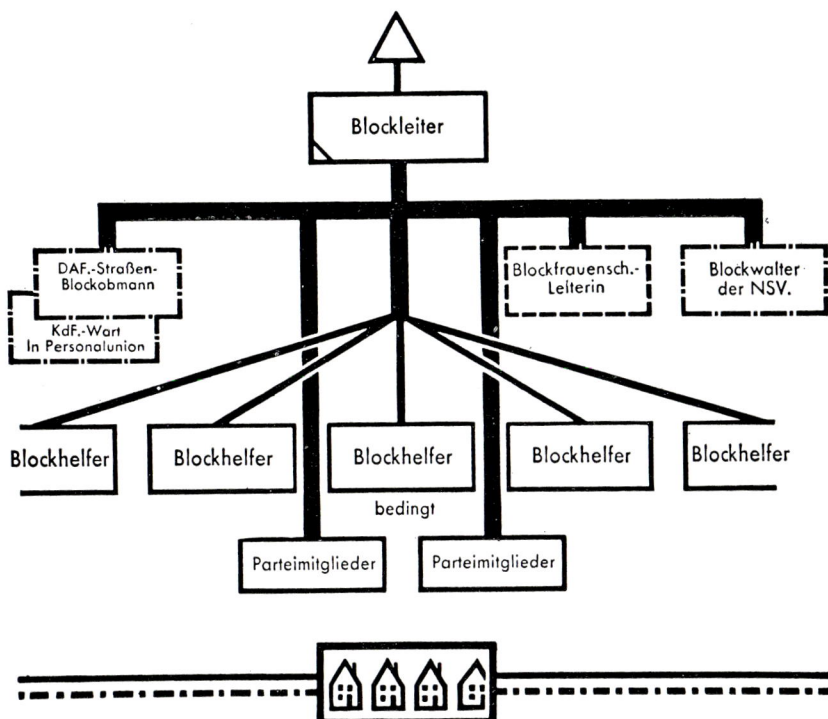

```
                          △
                          │
                    ┌───────────┐
                    │ Blockleiter│◸
                    └───────────┘
```

| DAF.-Straßen-Blockobmann | | Blockfrauensch.-Leiterin | Blockwalter der NSV. |

| KdF.-Wart In Personalunion |

| Blockhelfer | Blockhelfer | Blockhelfer | Blockhelfer | Blockhelfer |

bedingt

| Parteimitglieder | Parteimitglieder |

Zeichen-Erklärung

Reichsleiter	Reichsleitung
Hauptdienstleiter	Gauleitung
Gauleiter	Kreisleitung
Stellvertr. Gauleiter	Ortsgruppe
Kreisleiter	Zelle
Ortsgruppenleiter	Block
Zellenleiter	
Blockleiter	

E. Überſicht über Dienſtſtellenſchilder

I. Hoheitsſchilder

𝔑r. 1 a

b

Der
Reichsschatzmeister

𝔑r. 2 a

b

Gauleitung
Pommern

𝔑r. 3 a

b

Kreisleitung
Greifswald

𝔑r. 4 a

b

Ortsgruppe
Greifswald-Mitte

𝔑r. 5 a

*Official patterns for signs
and nameplates used in
the NSDAP.*

b

Auslands-
Organisation
Landesgruppenleitung
in Italien

66

II. Hauptschilder

Nr. 6 a

b

Nr. 7 a

b

Nr. 8 a

b

Nr. 9 a

b

Nr. 10 a

b

Nr. 11 a

b

Nr. 12 a

b

Nr. 13 a

b

Nr. 14 a

b

Nr. 15 a

b

Nr. 16a

b

Nr. 17a

b

Nr. 18a

b

Nr. 19a

b

III. Wohnungstürschilder

The GAUE of the NSDAP

The GAUE of the NSDAP consists of altogether 920
Party Kreise, including the territories of Alsace, Lorraine,
Luxembourg, Upper Carniola, Lower Styria and Balystok.

Gau No.	Gau	Seat	Party Kreise
1	Baden	Karlsruhe	39
2	Bayreuth	Bayreuth	40
3	Berlin	Berlin W9	10
4	Danzig-Wesipr.	Danzig	28
5	Düsseldorf	Düsseldorf	7
6	Essen	Essen	9
7	Franken	Nürnberg-O.	11

Gau No.	Gau	Seat	Party Kreise
8	Halle-Merseburg	Halle/Saale	17
9	Hamburg	Hamburg 36	10
10	Hessen-Nassau	Frankfurt a.M.	26
11	Kärnten	Klagenfurt	11
12	Köln-Aachen	Köln a.Rhein	18
13	Kurhessen	Kassel	15
14	Magdeburg-Anhalt	Dessau	18
15	Mainfranken	Würzburg	14
16	Mark Brandenburg	Berlin W35	30
17	Mecklenburg	Schwerin	13
18	Moselland	Koblenz	22
19	München-Obb.	München	21
20	Niederdonau	Wien IX	26
21	Niederschlesien	Breslau	35
22	Oberdonau	Linz	17
23	Oberschlesien	Kattowitz	26
24	Osthannover	Lüneburg	16
25	Ostpreußen	Königsberg	45
26	Pommern	Stettin	31
27	Sachsen	Dresden A1	27
28	Salzburg	Salzburg	5
29	Schleswig-Holst.	Kiel	21
30	Schwaben	Augsburg	15
31	Steiermark	Graz	24
32	Sudetenland	Reichenberg	45
33	Süd.-Hann.-Braunschweig	Hannover	27
34	Thüringen	Weimar	20
35	Tirol-Vorarlberg	Innsbruck	10
36	Wartheland	Posen	40
37	Weser-Ems	Oldenburg	23
38	Westf.-Nord	Münster i.W.	19
39	Westf.-Süd	Bochum	18
40	Westmark	Neustadt. a.d.W.	26
41	Wien	Wien 1	10
42	Würtiemb.-Hohenzollern	Stuttgart	35
43	Auslandsorganisation	Berlin	

NOTES

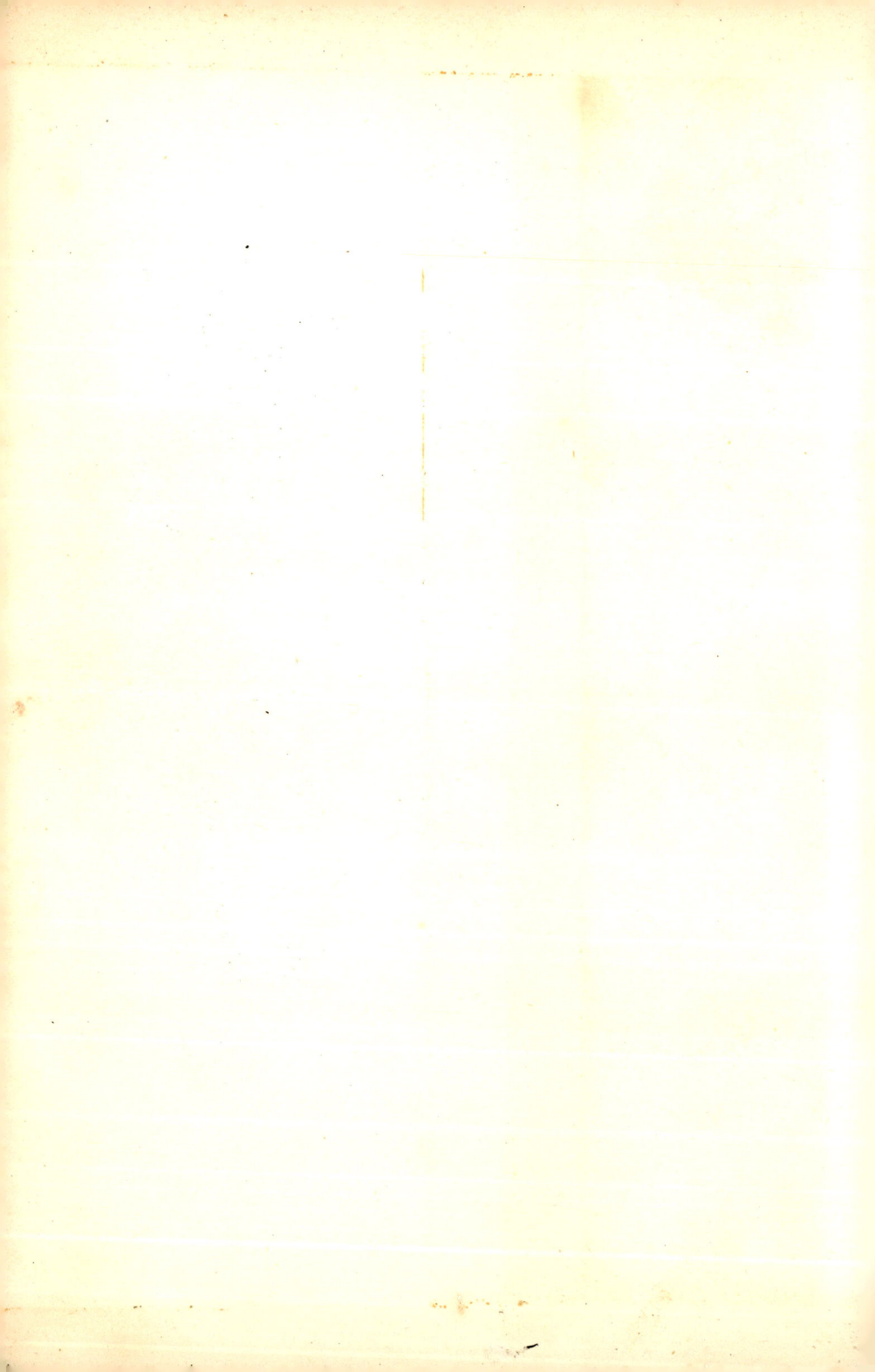